Constantinople 1453

The end of Byzantium

OSPREY
PUBLISHING

Constantinople 1453

The end of Byzantium

David Nicolle · Illustrated by Christa Hook

Series editor Lee Johnson · Consultant editor David G Chandler

First published in Great Britain in 2000 by Osprey Publishing, Elms Court,
Chapel Way, Botley, Oxford OX2 9LP United Kingdom
Email: info@ospreypublishing.com

ISBN 1 84176 091 9

Consultant Editor: DAVID G. CHANDLER
Series Editor: LEE JOHNSON

Editor: Judith Millidge
Design: Ken Vail Graphic Design, Cambridge, UK
Colour bird's-eye-view illustrations by the Black Spot
Cartography by The Map Studio
Battlescene artwork by Christa Hook
Originated by Grasmere Digital Imaging, Leeds, UK
Printed in China through World Print Ltd

02 03 04   10 9 8 7 6 5 4 3 2

FOR A CATALOGUE OF ALL BOOKS PUBLISHED BY
OSPREY MILITARY AND AVIATION PLEASE CONTACT:

The Marketing Manager, Osprey Direct UK,
PO Box 140, Wellingborough, Northants,
NN8 2FA, United Kingdom.
Email: info@ospreydirect.co.uk

The Marketing Manager, Osprey Direct USA,
c/o MBI Publishing, PO Box 1,
729 Prospect Avenue, Osceola, WI 54020, USA.
Email: info@ospreydirectusa.com

www.ospreypublishing.com

Dedication

For Brendan
Once more unto the breach, but this time on a skateboard.

Artist's Note

Readers may care to note that the original paintings from
which the colour plates in this book were prepared are
available for private sale. All reproduction copyright
whatsoever is retained by the publisher. All enquiries
should be addressed to:

Scorpio Gallery
P.O. Box 475
Hailsham
East Sussex
BN27 2SL
UK

The publishers regret that they can enter into no
correspondence on this matter.

FRONT COVER: The siege of Constantinople 1453 by unknown artist, detail of Turks
killing Christians. (© The Art Archive/Moldovita Monastery Rumania)

KEY TO MILITARY SYMBOLS

CONTENTS

THE ORIGINS OF THE CAMPAIGN

The fall of Constantinople to the Ottoman Turks in 1453 is sometimes regarded as the end of the Roman Empire, or as the absorption of a redundant relic by a new and expansionist superstate. In reality, the siege and conquest of Constantinople was neither; nor was it such a one-sided affair as it might seem. The real importance of 1453 lies not in the disappearance of something ancient, but in the birth of something new: the Ottoman Empire in its fully developed form, an empire which would endure until 1922.

To the Ottomans the Balkans were *Rum-eli*, Rumelia, 'the land of the Romans'. They looked upon it as the Spanish Conquistadores regarded America: as a land where the conquerors had a free hand, where the local people were ripe for conversion, and where conqueror society was dominated by the masculine virtues of courage and fortitude. By the mid-15th century, however, the Ottoman élite was divided between those who clung to the old heroic ideal of autonomous *ghazi*, (religiously inspired) frontier warfare, and those in favour of a new military and administrative centralisation. Whereas the feudal élite generally opposed

7

centralisation, the *Kapi Kulu,* or 'slaves of the gate', favoured a concentration of power around the sultan. Although the *Kapi Kulu* were theoretically slaves, many were free-born, and proudly claimed the title of *Kul.* This might best be described as 'sultan's man', and Sultan Mehmet II, the conqueror of Constantinople, had advisers from both traditions.

The conquest of the Byzantine capital had been a dream of Islamic armies ever since their first assaults in the 8th century. Alongside such Islamic motivation, the Turks focused their own dream of the *Kizil-Elma,* or 'Red Apple' to which destiny led the Turks, upon Constantinople. Sultan Mehmet II and his immediate predecessors had adopted the title of *Sultan-i Rum,* 'ruler of the Romans' and thus claimed to be the heirs of Byzantium and Rome. In fact Ottoman Turks were often called *Rumiyun* by Muslims further east.

The last Byzantines also called themselves 'Romans', but their emperors held very little territory. The remaining lands, however, could serve as naval bases for the Ottomans' powerful maritime rivals in Italy,

Portalan maps like this one dating from 1413 were made for sailors, and paid little attention to inland features. Venetian and Genoese islands are shown darker than the mainland, while Constantinople at the upper-centre is marked by two flags indicating the Byzantine capital and Genoese Galata. (Hocia de Villadeste Portalan Map, Res. Ge AA 566, Bibliothèque Nationale, Paris)

The Anadolu Hisari fortress was built on the eastern (Asiatic) shore of the Bosphorus by Sultan Bayezit I in 1390–91. It was relatively small but provided Ottoman forces with a secure base from which to send troops across the Bosphorus. (Author's photograph)

while the only major European power facing the Ottomans on land was Hungary. In 1444 the Ottoman Empire had almost been cut in two by a combined naval and land Crusade. Even the Byzantine *Despot* of the Morea in southern Greece, the future Emperor Constantine XI, had struck northwards into Ottoman and vassal lands. For Mehmet II, who became sultan aged 12 in July 1444 when his father, Murad II, abdicated, the events of that year were a personal humiliation. The Grand Vizier, Çandarli Halil, convinced Murad to return, defeated the Hungarians at Varna and forced the Byzantines back. Two years later Murad formally reassumed the title of sultan while young Mehmet was sent to govern a small Anatolian province. Mehmet II may have smarted from his temporary deposition, but he also noted that his father's army crossed the Bosphorus under the protection of guns which held back the Christian galleys. It was a lesson well learned, for on this same spot Mehmet subsequently built the great fortress of Rumeli Hisar.

To the Ottomans, the Byzantine emperor was merely the *Tekfur*, an Armenian term for king, while his great city of Constantinople was a pale shadow of its former self. In fact, the emperor was a vassal of the Ottoman sultan, as were his subordinates, the *Despots* of the Morea. The sultan's capital was Edirne, in Thrace, some 100 miles (160km) west of Constantinople. Far to the east, the Byzantine Empire of Trebizond (Trabzon) was a separate state ruled by a rival dynasty, while to the north the little Byzantine principality of Mangoup in the Crimea was little more than an offshoot of the Genoese colonies on the Crimean coast. Venice and Genoa dominated the seas and controlled most of the islands as well as several coastal enclaves around the Aegean and Black seas. The Black Sea was the crossroads of major trade routes linking Europe and Central Asia, Russia and the Middle East. At the centre was the Crimean peninsula, whose coasts were largely controlled by the Genoese. Venice and Genoa had also fought over the strategic north Aegean island of Tenedos (now Bozcaada) at the entrance to the Dardanelles.

The Crusader principality of Athens was ruled by a family of mixed Italian-Catalan origin who had links with the Aragonese rulers of southern Italy. But all that remained of the once powerful Byzantine

9

Despotate of Epirus were three coastal castles and the Ionian islands ruled by an Italian, Leonardo III Tocco. To the north, some Albanian clans recognised the leadership of George Kastriotes, better known as Skanderbeg, but he spent as much effort quarrelling with the Venetians as resisting the Ottomans.

To the east, Ottoman domination of what is now Turkey was far from complete. In northern Anatolia the Candar Oghullari of Sinop were loyal vassals of the Ottoman sultan, but to the south the Karamanids only accepted Ottoman overlordship unwillingly. Beyond the Black Sea, part of the immense Mongol Golden Horde had broken away when Hajji Girei created what became the vigorous Khanate of Krim (Crimea). The Catholic kingdom of Poland-Lithuania had also taken control of vast regions of Orthodox Christian Russia, including part of the Black Sea

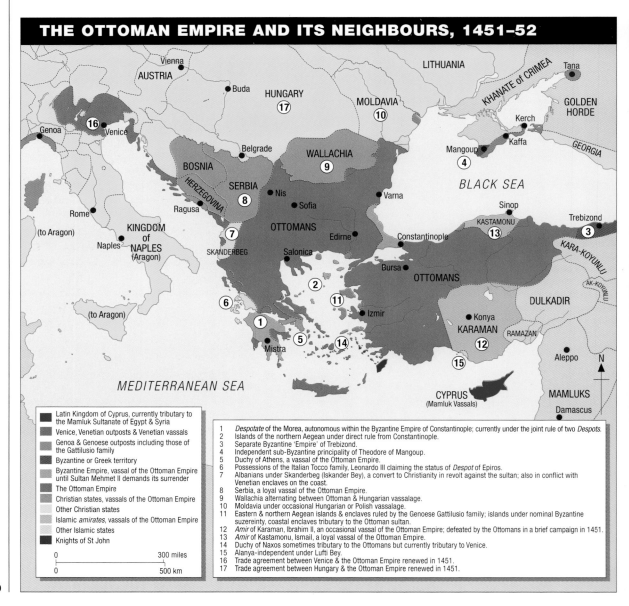

THE OTTOMAN EMPIRE AND ITS NEIGHBOURS, 1451–52

Latin Kingdom of Cyprus, currently tributary to the Mamluk Sultanate of Egypt & Syria
Venice, Venetian outposts & Venetian vassals
Genoa & Genoese outposts including those of the Gattilusio family
Byzantine or Greek territory
Byzantine Empire, vassal of the Ottoman Empire until Sultan Mehmet II demands its surrender
The Ottoman Empire
Christian states, vassals of the Ottoman Empire
Other Christian states
Islamic *amirates*, vassals of the Ottoman Empire
Other Islamic states
Knights of St John

0   300 miles
0   500 km

1   *Despotate* of the Morea, autonomous within the Byzantine Empire of Constantinople; currently under the joint rule of two *Despots*.
2   Islands of the northern Aegean under direct rule from Constantinople.
3   Separate Byzantine 'Empire' of Trebizond.
4   Independent sub-Byzantine principality of Theodore of Mangoup.
5   Duchy of Athens, a vassal of the Ottoman Empire.
6   Possessions of the Italian Tocco family, Leonardo III claiming the status of *Despot* of Epiros.
7   Albanians under Skanderbeg (Iskander Bey), a convert to Christianity in revolt against the sultan; also in conflict with Venetian enclaves on the coast.
8   Serbia, a loyal vassal of the Ottoman Empire.
9   Wallachia alternating between Ottoman & Hungarian vassalage.
10   Moldavia under occasional Hungarian or Polish vassalage.
11   Eastern & northern Aegean islands & enclaves ruled by the Genoese Gattilusio family; islands under nominal Byzantine suzereinty, coastal enclaves tributary to the Ottoman sultan.
12   *Amir* of Karaman, Ibrahim II, an occasional vassal of the Ottoman Empire; defeated by the Ottomans in a brief campaign in 1451.
13   *Amir* of Kastamonu, Ismail, a loyal vassal of the Ottoman Empire.
14   Duchy of Naxos sometimes tributary to the Ottomans but currently tributary to Venice.
15   Alanya-independent under Lufti Bey.
16   Trade agreement between Venice & the Ottoman Empire renewed in 1451.
17   Trade agreement between Hungary & the Ottoman Empire renewed in 1451.

ABOVE *The Martyrdom of
St Demetrios* on a 15th-century
Byzantine icon. This icon
contains some interesting and
realistic features, including the
varied helmets, typically
European straight swords and a
Balkan rectangular shield.
(Benaki Museum, inv. 2980,
Athens)

ABOVE RIGHT *The Resurrection*
on a Transylvanian painted
altarback dating from 1480–90.
The soldiers reflect Balkan
troops such as those who fought
both for and against the
Ottomans during the siege of
Constantinople. (*in situ* Lutheran
Church, Medias)

coast. Russia had little real interest in the affairs of Orthodox
Constantinople and recently the Metropolitan of Moscow declared the
Church of Russia to be autonomous, effectively turning its back upon
Byzantium.

While most Christian countries were concerned with their own
affairs, Mehmet II's determination to conquer Constantinople became
clear as soon as he returned to the throne in 1451. Though not yet
strong enough to remove the cautious old Grand Vizier Çandarli Halil,
the young sultan promoted his own closest advisers Zaganos Pasha and
Shihab al-Din Pasha as the Second and Third Viziers respectively. He also
showed a streak of ruthlessness by having his younger brother Küçük
Ahmet killed, thus removing a potential focus of discontent. This still left
another claimant to the Ottoman throne, Prince Orhan, who lived in
Constantinople like a political refugee.

The Byzantine emperor and the ruler of Karaman both regarded
Sultan Mehmet II as an inexperienced youth. But Mehmet and his
warlike advisers had already decided that a great victory was needed to
secure their position. The conquest of Constantinople would also stop
any Crusade from using the city as a base and would prevent
Constantinople being handed over to a dangerous western European
rival. Mehmet II summed up the situation simply and succinctly: 'The
ghaza [Holy War] is our basic duty as it was in the case of our fathers.
Constantinople, situated in the middle of our domains, protects our
enemies and incites them against us. The conquest of this city is,

therefore, essential to the future and the safety of the Ottoman state.'

Shortly after Mehmet II came to the throne for the second time, Ibrahim Bey of Karaman invaded the disputed Hamid-ili region, but it took only a brief campaign to teach Ibrahim that the young sultan was not to be trifled with. The Byzantine Emperor Constantine XI also thought Mehmet ineffective and tried to extract concessions by threatening to let Prince Orhan stir up an Ottoman civil war. Instead, Mehmet married Ibrahim Bey's daughter and returned home more determined to crush Constantinople. Even Çandarli Halil's impatience boiled over. 'You stupid Greeks,' he blurted out, 'I have known your cunning ways long enough. The late Sultan (Murad) was a tolerant and conscientious friend of yours. The present Sultan Mehmet is not of the same mind. If Constantinople eludes his bold and impetuous grasp it will only be because God continues to overlook your devious and wicked schemes.'

On his way back to Edirne, the sultan's passage across the Dardanelles was blocked by Christian ships so he crossed via the Bosphorus, and it was this journey that apparently prompted Mehmet to built a massive fortress on the European shore. Once back in Edirne, the sultan took control of the Janissary infantry away from Çandarli Halil and placed his own *devsirme*, 'slave recruited', officers in command of other infantry units. Çandarli Halil even feared for his life since many in court referred to him as a friend of the infidels, but Mehmet could not afford to oust the powerful old politician. Sultan Mehmet and his closest advisers also walked around Edirne at night dressed as common soldiers and listened to talk in the taverns to assess the popularity of his proposed attack upon Constantinople.

Meanwhile, Emperor Constantine sent out urgent pleas for assistance. On 14 February 1452 the Venetian Senate answered with excuses and a promise to send military supplies. Many Venetian senators already regarded Byzantium as a lost cause and favoured improving relations with the Ottomans. Aware of such mixed feelings, Çandarli Halil blunted Constantine's appeals for aid by renewing various agreements with Venice, Hungary and the vassal states of Serbia and Wallachia.

Orders had already been despatched in 1451 to collect materials and craftsmen for the building of Rumeli Hisar, while in Constantinople people cried: 'These are the days of the Anti-Christ. This is the end of the city.' The Emperor Constantine complained that the sultan had not asked permission to build his castle within Byzantine territory, but Mehmet merely replied that the area was uninhabited and that Constantine owned nothing outside the walls of Constantinople.

In order to build Rumeli Hisar, Mehmet II needed a fleet powerful enough to stop outside interference. The sudden appearance of an Ottoman fleet of six war galleys, 18 smaller *galliots* and 16 supply ships from Gallipoli took the Christians by surprise. Work began in April 1452 where the Bosphorus was at its narrowest, about 88 metres across; 500 workmen completed the great triangular fortress by 31 August 1452. The work was not without incident, however. There were brawls between

A Milanese armour with a painted salet helmet, again made in the mid-15th century. (Scott Collection, Glasgow Museums and Art Galleries)

An Italian armour made in Milan for Galeazzo d'Arco in 1440-50. (formerly Trapp Collection, Churburg Castle)

Ottoman soldiers and local Byzantine peasants, mostly over grain supplies as the Emperor Constantine wanted all available food to be stockpiled inside Constantinople. Some eunuchs who worked in the sultan's harem strayed too close to Constantinople and were arrested, but begged to be released because their heads would be forfeit if they failed to turn up for duty on time.

The Turks called Rumeli Hisar '*Bogaz kesen*', the Greeks, '*Laimokopia*'; both phrases meant 'cutter of the Straits' or 'of the throat'. It was immediately garrisoned by 400 men under Firuz Bey, whose duty was to impose a toll on all passing ships. Those which refused would be fired upon and if possible sunk by cannon along the shore. The biggest gun reportedly fired a ball weighting 600 lb (272 kg) and surviving cannonballs at Rumeli Hisar certainly weigh 450 pounds (204 kg).

Sultan Mehmet now returned to Edirne and the Ottoman fleet under Baltaoglu Sulayman Bey left a week later. During the autumn of 1452 troops from the Rumelian provinces set up camp next to the élite palace regi-ments around Edirne. Armourers were hard at work throughout the state, while the sultan studied the latest military ideas from east and west. One of his advisers appears to have been a famous Italian scholar, traveller and collector of ancient antiquities, Ciriaco de Pizzicolli, better known as 'Ciriaco of Ancona'. Among other experts attracted to Mehmet II's court was a Hungarian gunfounder named Urban, who had left Byzantine employment because the emperor could not or would not supply him with the necessary funds and materials. When asked if he could make cannon to break the walls of Constantinople, Urban replied yes, although he admitted that as a gunmaker rather than artilleryman he was not qualified to work out ranges for the cannon at Rumeli Hisar. Mehmet II offered whatever Urban needed and said that ranges could be sorted out later.

It took two months to make the guns for Rumeli Hisar, but on 10 November they opened fire on a pair of Venetian ships returning from the Black Sea. The Italian crews had a fright but reached Constantinople safely. The Ottoman gunners adjusted their ranges and on 25 November sunk a Venetian ship commanded by Antonio Erizzo. When Sultan Mehmet heard the news he ordered Urban to make a cannon twice the size of the first and capable of shooting a ball weighing over 1,000 pounds (450kg). This was eventually tested outside the sultan's new palace and duly shot a massive stone cannonball over a mile.

In the face of these overt preparations, Emperor Constantine brought food supplies, wine and even winnowing fans into Constantinople, along with people from outlying villages. During the winter of 1452–53 he also sent ships to the Aegean to purchase food and military equipment. One particularly large ship was trapped by contrary winds at Chios and could not sail homeward until after the siege began. Throughout the winter the defences of Constantinople were improved and silver was taken from churches and monasteries to pay the troops.

Many in the city maintained that only God and the Virgin could now save Constantinople, and that it was folly for the emperor to flirt with the schismatic Catholic western Europeans. Little more than warm words

had been supplied by the West so far. The separate Byzantine Empire of Trebizond was preoccupied with its own problems, while in the Morea the co-*Despots* Demetrios and Thomas faced a substantial raid by Ottoman troops in October 1452. During this operation, Byzantine troops under Matthew Asanes captured a senior Ottoman leader, Ahmad Bey, but this could not alter the fact that no help for Constantinople would come from this area. The remaining Latin enclaves in Greece were too weak to do anything, and it was the same in the Balkans, where the *Despot* George of Serbia would support his Ottoman overlord. According to the Byzantine chronicler George Sphrantzes, the great Hungarian military leader Janos Hunyadi had demanded Mesembria or Selymbria in return for helping Constantinople. Sphrantzes also claimed that the Aegean island of Lemnos was given to King Alfonso V of Aragon to use as a naval base from which to help Constantinople. Nothing came from either of these remarkable proposals. Turkish rulers in Anatolia were either friendly towards the Ottomans or were frightened of them.

Following the sinking of their ship in the Bosphorus, the Venetians were concerned how to protect their merchant convoys to the Black Sea. Gabriele Trevisan, the Vice-Captain of the Gulf, was sent back to Constantinople, where his ships and crews were to help defend the city if necessary. The Senate also decided to arm two transports, each carrying 400 soldiers and accompanied by 15 galleys to sail for Constantinople on 8 April. The Venetian authorities in Crete would similarly send two warships to Negroponte to be placed under the command of Zaccaria Grioni, recently arrived from the Byzantine capital. The command structure was then changed and the fleet for Constantinople was put under Giacomo Loredan, the Captain-General of the Sea, who was already on his way east and was now ordered to wait at Modon for the galleys commanded by Alvise Longo. Further delays followed, and Longo was told to take his fleet to Constantinople and place himself under the Venetian *baillie* (local consul), Minotto, until Loredan arrived. In the event Alvise Longo set sail from Venice on 19 April with only one warship, while the main Venetian fleet, which eventually assembled in the Aegean, was too late to help Constantinople. It is important to remember that it took at least a month for a message to travel between Constantinople and Venice via Negroponte and Corfu.

Meanwhile, the Venetians in Constantinople had to decide what to do. Girolomo Minotto, the *baillie*, persuaded Trevisan to remain under his command. Other Venetian merchants, captains, crews and soldiers were in the city, including Giacomo Coco, who captained of one of the ships which had run the gauntlet past Rumeli Hisar. In December Minotto summoned a meeting of his council with the Emperor Constantine present, and the leading Venetians voted to stay. No ship would be allowed to leave without the *baillie*'s permission, but on 26 February 1453 six ships defied Minotto's orders and fled, carrying 700 people.

In Rome the Pope saw Constantinople's predicament as an opportunity to convince the Greek Orthodox Church to accept union

A replica galleon sails past the ruins of the 13th-century Byzantine castle of Anadolu Kavagi, indicating the vulnerability of ships in the Bosphorus to Sultan Mehmet's powerful new artillery at Rumeli Hisari. (Author's photograph)

LEFT The Rumeli Hisari fortress was built for Sultan Mehmet II in 1452 on the European shore of the Bosphorus. With its big cannon it could close the straits to ships sailing between the Black Sea and Constantinople. (Author's photograph)

RIGHT The sketch plan of the newly built Rumeli Hisari was made by an anonymous Venetian in 1453. Just below a crease in the paper, six large cannon are lined up along the shore, while on the other side of the Bosphorus the older Anadolu Hisari appears as a smaller castle. (Biblioteca Trivulziana, Cod. membranaceo 641, Milan)

OPPOSITE MIDDLE LEFT A late 15th-century cannon made of wrought iron staves surrounded by wrought iron hoops, Mamluk or Ottoman. (Askeri Müze, Istanbul; Author's photograph)

OPPOSITE MIDDLE RIGHT A bronze Ottoman cannon with the narrower powder chamber shown in many 15th-century pictures. (Askeri Müze, Istanbul)

OPPOSITE BOTTOM LEFT The difference in bore of the barrel and powder chamber of this 15th-century Hungarian wrought iron gun is more obvious. (National Museum, Budapest; Author's photograph.

OPPOSITE BOTTOM RIGHT This small bronze cannon was almost certainly made in Venice then sold to the Ottoman sultan's eastern neighbour and rival, the emir of Karaman in the 15th century. (Historical Museum, Karaman; author's photograph)

with the Roman Catholic Church. So Cardinal Isidore was sent to the Byzantine capital in a Venetian galley, arriving in November 1452. He brought some archers and hand-gunners from Naples and enlisted more troops at Chios, where he was joined by Archbishop Leonard. In Constantinople Cardinal Isidore's 200 soldiers were regarded as the advance guard of a great army which would save the city. On 12 December a Unionate service was held in the ancient church of Santa Sofia and the leaders of the Orthodox Church agreed to a Decree of Union. Unfortunately, most of the ordinary Orthodox clergy and large numbers of the common people disagreed, and there was widespread rioting led by a monk named Gennadius. He subsequently become the first Orthodox Patriarch appointed by Sultan Mehmet.

In November 1452 Venice's great rival, Genoa, decided to send help and in January 1453 Giovanni Giustiniani Longo arrived in the Golden Horn with 700 troops. The Byzantine chronicler Doukas described them as 'two huge ships which were carrying a large supply of excellent military equipment and well-armed youthful Genoese soldiers full of martial passion'. Longo's reputation was such that Constantine put him in charge of all land forces with the rank of *protostrator* (marshal) and gave him the island of Lemnos as a reward for his services.

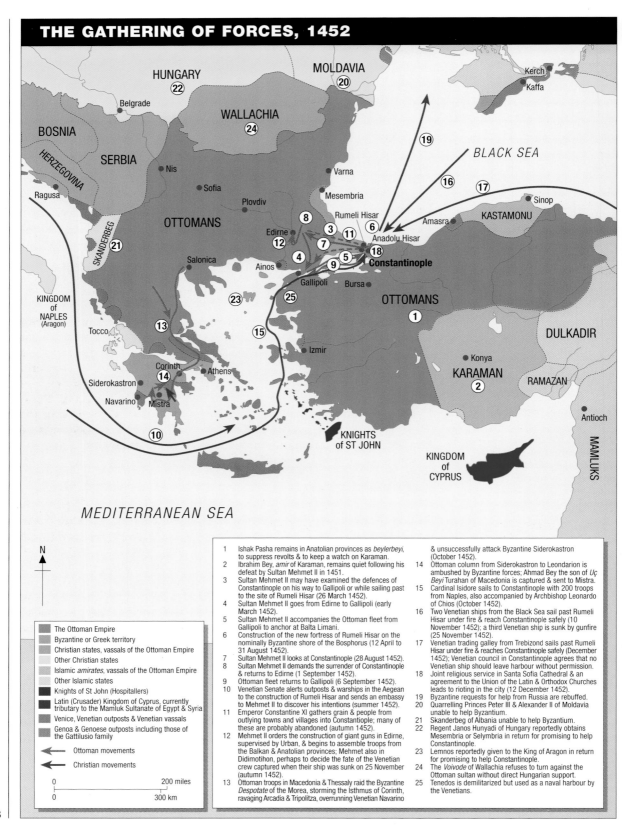

1 Ishak Pasha remains in Anatolian provinces as *beylerbeyi*, to suppress revolts & to keep a watch on Karaman.

2 Ibrahim Bey, *amir* of Karaman, remains quiet following his defeat by Sultan Mehmet II in 1451.

3 Sultan Mehmet II may have examined the defences of Constantinople on his way to Gallipoli or while sailing past to the site of Rumeli Hisar (26 March 1452).

4 Sultan Mehmet II goes from Edirne to Gallipoli (early March 1452).

5 Sultan Mehmet II accompanies the Ottoman fleet from Gallipoli to anchor at Balta Limani.

6 Construction of the new fortress of Rumeli Hisar on the nominally Byzantine shore of the Bosphorus (12 April to 31 August 1452).

7 Sultan Mehmet II looks at Constantinople (28 August 1452).

8 Sultan Mehmet II demands the surrender of Constantinople & returns to Edirne (1 September 1452).

9 Ottoman fleet returns to Gallipoli (6 September 1452).

10 Venetian Senate alerts outposts & warships in the Aegean to the construction of Rumeli Hisar and sends an embassy to Mehmet II to discover his intentions (summer 1452).

11 Emperor Constantine XI gathers grain & people from outlying towns and villages into Constantiople; many of these are probably abandoned (autumn 1452).

12 Mehmet II orders the construction of giant guns in Edirne, supervised by Urban, & begins to assemble troops from the Balkan & Anatolian provinces; Mehmet also in Didimothon, perhaps to decide the fate of the Venetian crew captured when their ship was sunk on 25 November (autumn 1452).

13 Ottoman troops in Macedonia & Thessaly raid the Byzantine *Despotate* of the Morea, storming the Isthmus of Corinth, ravaging Arcadia & Tripolitza, overrunning Venetian Navarino

& unsuccessfully attack Byzantine Siderokastron (October 1452).

14 Ottoman column from Siderokastron to Leondarion is ambushed by Byzantine forces; Ahmad Bey the son of *Uç Beyi* Turahan of Macedonia is captured & sent to Mistra.

15 Cardinal Isidore sails to Constantinople with 200 troops from Naples, also accompanied by Archbishop Leonardo of Chios (October 1452).

16 Two Venetian ships from the Black Sea sail past Rumeli Hisar under fire & reach Constantinople safely (10 November 1452); a third Venetian ship is sunk by gunfire (25 November 1452).

17 Venetian trading galley from Trebizond sails past Rumeli Hisar safely & reaches Constantinople safely (December 1452); Venetian council in Constantinople agrees that no Venetian ship should leave harbour without permission.

18 Joint religious service in Santa Sofia Cathedral & an agreement to the Union of the Latin & Orthodox Churches leads to rioting in the city (12 December 1452).

19 Byzantine requests for help from Russia are rebuffed.

20 Quarrelling Princes Peter III & Alexander II of Moldavia unable to help Byzantium.

21 Skanderbeg of Albania unable to help Byzantium.

22 Regent Janos Hunyadi of Hungary reportedly obtains Mesembria or Selymbria in return for promising to help Constantinople.

23 Lemnos reportedly given to the King of Aragon in return for promising to help Constantinople.

24 The *Voivode* of Wallachia refuses to turn against the Ottoman sultan without direct Hungarian support.

25 Tenedos is demilitarized but used as a naval harbour by the Venetians.

The Ottoman Empire

Byzantine or Greek territory

Christian states, vassals of the Ottoman Empire

Other Christian states

Islamic *amirates*, vassals of the Ottoman Empire

Other Islamic states

Knights of St John (Hospitallers)

Latin (Crusader) Kingdom of Cyprus, currently tributary to the Mamluk Sultanate of Egypt & Syria

Venice, Venetian outposts & Venetian vassals

Genoa & Genoese outposts including those of the Gattilusio family

Ottoman movements

Christian movements

0   200 miles

0   300 km

OPPOSING COMMANDERS

OTTOMAN LEADERS

Sultan Mehmet II was the fourth son of Murad II, and was born at Edirne on 30 March 1432. His mother was Murad's first wife, a Turkish woman possibly named Huma Hatun. At the age of 11 Mehmet was sent with his two *lalas* or advisers to govern the province of Amasya. As a young man he had full pink cheeks, a firm red mouth, a blond moustache and a hooked nose. Around 1450 he married Sitt Khatun, daughter of the Dulkadir ruler and a traditional ally of the Ottomans in eastern Anatolia.

Mehmet also had a strong interest in ancient Greek and medieval Byzantine civilisation. His heroes were Achilles and Alexander the Great and he could discuss the Christian religion with some authority. As sultan, Mehmet II became a leading patron of Ottoman literature and built many *madrasa*, schools. In addition to his nickname of *Fathi,* 'the Conqueror', he was also known as *Abu'l-Khayrat* or 'Father of Good Works', providing pensions for no less than 30 Ottoman poets as well as others abroad. He was a poet himself, writing under the pseudonym of Avni and showing a romantic streak in such *gazals* (verses) as:

I asked her, why across your cheeks,
So disordered roam your tresses?
It is Rum-eli, she replied,
Why high starred heroes gallop.

The senior figures who supported Mehmet II during the Constantinople campaign included men of very differing characters and backgrounds. Çandarli Halil came from a Turkish family, probably based in Iznik, which provided five Grand Viziers to several early Ottoman rulers. The close but ultimately fatal links between the Çandarlis and the Byzantine court began under Çandarli Halil's father, Ibrahim, himself the son of Ali Pasha Çandarli, who served Bayazit I so well (see Campaign 64, *Nicopolis 1396*). Çandarli Ibrahim Pasha was also the first to follow the cautious military policy which characterised the reign of Murad II. Ibrahim's eldest son, Çandarli Halil, became Grand Vizier in 1443, continuing his father's cautious line and serving both Murad II and Mehmet II until his execution after the fall of Constantinople.

Though he came from a legal and religious background, Çandarli Halil enjoyed the support of the Janissary corps and probably deserved most of the credit for defeating the Hungarians at the close-run battle of Varna in 1444. Although many in the Byzantine governing élite regarded Çandarli Halil as a friend, stories of his collaboration with the Byzantines during the Constantinople campaign were probably spread by the rival war-faction led by Zaganos Pasha. In fact Çandarli Halil fell from favour immediately after Constantinople fell and was executed soon afterwards.

One of his sons, Ibrahim Pasha, became *qadi* or judge of Edirne in 1453 and remained in office despite his father's disgrace, being appointed *Qadi'askar* or chief judge of the army in 1465 and subsequently a *lala* or tutor-adviser to Prince Bayazid. When Prince Bayazid became sultan, Çandarli Ibrahim Pasha steady rose in rank to become Grand Vizier in 1498. Unfortunately there seems to be no information about Çandarli Halil's grave, though his father and grandfather are buried in a fine tomb at Iznik; Çandarli Ibrahim is also buried in that town. Sadly, these fine Ottoman monuments were damaged by Greek invaders in 1921.

Zaganos Pasha was a very different man, in both background and character. He is believed to have been of 'Illyrian' or Albanian origin, recruited into the Ottoman military establishment through the *devsirme* as a young slave or prisoner-of-war. A committed convert to Islam, Zaganos was above all a soldier who believed that the Ottoman state must continually expand to keep its enemies off balance. He was absolutely loyal to Mehmet, both as prince and later as sultan, knowing that his own prospects depended upon his patron's success. Zaganos accompanied the young Sultan Mehmet into effective exile in 1446 and when Mehmet II returned to the throne, Zaganos Pasha was rewarded with the rank of Second Vizier, and eventually replaced Çandarli Halil as Grand Vizier. In 1456, however, Zaganos Pasha was made the scapegoat following an unsuccessful expedition against Hungarian-held Belgrade. His daughter was expelled from the sultan's harem and both were banished to Balikesir, where Zaganos probably owned property. In 1459 Zaganos Pasha returned to become *Kapudan Pasha* or admiral of the fast-expanding Ottoman navy, then governor of Thessaly and Macedonia the following year. A mosque in the town of Balikesir was endowed by Zaganos Pasha around 1454 and now contains his tomb as well as those of other members of his family.

As leader of the relatively new Ottoman navy, Baltaoglu Suleyman Bey ranked lower than many other commanders and little is known about

him. He was the son of a Bulgarian *boyar* or aristocrat, and was almost certainly recruited into the Ottoman *Kapi Kulu* as a prisoner-of-war. Baltaoglu first caught Mehmet II's attention in 1444 when the young sultan made him part of an embassy to the Hungarian capital. Five years later, as an officer in the Ottoman fleet, Baltaoglu led a successful attack on the Genoese-ruled island of Lesbos. Baltaoglu may also have been governor of Gallipoli. According to the Byzantine chronicler Doukas, 'When he was enslaved by Mehmet's father he renounced the religion of his fathers. He had come to Lesbos four years earlier [than the siege of Constantinople] and taken many captives. He was not a good friend of those brigands the Janissaries because he often seized their spoils.'

By the siege of Constantinople Baltaoglu was *Kapudan Pasha*, Commander of the Fleet; the first man to hold this rank. Baltaoglu Suleyman Bey was undoubtedly stripped of his rank following his fleet's failure to stop Christian supply ships breaking through to Constantinople and he then seems to have disappeared from history. One source, however, mentions Baltaoglu commanding a Janissary unit during the final Ottoman assault. Perhaps Sultan Mehmet offered him the chance to redeem his reputation at the head of a forlorn hope. A village just north of Rumeli Hisar on the Bosphorus is called Balta Limani, or Balta's Harbour. Perhaps Baltaoglu retired there after the siege, though it is more likely that the name reflects the fact that the Ottoman fleet moored there whilst protecting the construction of Rumeli Hisar.

LEFT **A letter in Venetian Italian, dated 24 April 1480, and signed with Sultan Mehmet's *tugra* or official monogram. (Archico di Stato, Venice)**

BELOW **A silver medallion of Sultan Mehmet II as a young man. It was made for the Burgundian nobleman Jehan Tricaudet and is attributed to Matteo de Pasti. (Cabinet des Médailles, Bib. Nat., Paris)**

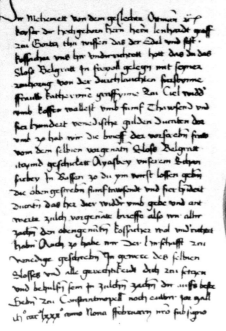

Among the few illustrated Ottoman manuscripts which survive from the late 15th century is a copy of the *Iskendername* or 'Epic of Alexander the Great' by Ahmedi. The book also includes events from early Ottoman history, such as this picture of the murder of Sultan Murad I by a Serbian. (Institute of Oriental Studies, Ms. C. 133, f.254a, St Petersburg)

CHRISTIAN LEADERS

The command structure in Constantinople was less clear cut than on the Ottoman side though Emperor Constantine XI Palaiologos was, of course, in overall authority. He was born into the ruling imperial family in Constantinople on 8 February 1405, the fourth son of Emperor Manuel II and his wife Helena Dragas. As a younger son he was sent to the Morea in southern Greece in 1428, to share the role of *Despot* with his brothers Theodore II and Thomas Palaiologos. As *Despot* the brave, energetic, but generally cautious Constantine strengthened local defences and even briefly reconquered Patras, Athens and Thebes.

Following the death of his childless elder brother, John VIII, *Despot* Constantine became Emperor Constantine XI on 12 March 1449, but was less effective as emperor than he had been as *Despot*. Flexible in religious matters and willing to accept Church Union, Constantine badly misjudged the domestic opposition within Byzantium and the unity of purpose within the Ottoman camp. Nevertheless, Constantine Palaiologos became a heroic figure in Greek legend, and following the fall of Constantinople many Greeks believed that their last emperor was not dead but had been turned to marble, ready to be awakened by an angel to drive out Turks. In its modernised version, as the *Megali Idea* ('Great Idea'), this legend would lead Greece to catastrophe in Turkey in the 1920s.

Like the emperor himself, Loukas Notaras was born in Constantinople. He was the son of a wealthy courtier who served as an interpreter for the Emperor Manuel and had been part of an embassy to France in 1398. Loukas' brother was also a courtier but had been killed during an earlier Ottoman attack upon Constantinople. As an important landowner in the Morea, Loukas had friends and contacts among the wealthy Italian merchants. So in addition to becoming a leading member of the emperor's government and a commander of troops, he was involved in trade and entrusted his own money to Italian bankers. Furthermore, Loukas Notaras became a citizen of both Venice and Genoa and married into the ruling Palaologos family.

With such wealth and connections, Loukas Notaras served three Byzantine emperors and shared the role of *Mesazon* or Chief Minister. From 1449 to the fall of Constantinople he was also *Megas Doux*, titular

The land-walls of Constantinople, now Istanbul, have been ravaged by war, earthquake and neglect. Nevertheless, they still tower over the western edge of the city. This stretch just north of the Golden Gate shows the inner wall with its square and octagonal towers, a lower outer wall with square and rounded towers, and the line of what would have been the outermost breastwork. The fosse or moat is marked by a broad line of green vegetation. (Author's photograph)

commander of the once mighty Byzantine navy. Pragmatic and flexible, but firmly opposed to a union of the Orthodox and Latin churches, Loukas Notaras had rivals, and one of them seems to have been the Byzantine politician Sphrantzes. He wrote that even Emperor Constantine XI once said: 'Notaras publicly and secretly maintains that no other affairs matter except his own and leaves no stone unturned, as the saying goes.' A eulogy written in 1470 sought to clear Loukas Notaras of the charges of treason against Constantinople in its final hours, and there is no evidence that this experienced and realistic political and military leader was in any real sense a traitor.

Apart from the tragic Emperor Constantine himself, the greatest Christian hero of the siege is probably Giovanni Giustiniani Longo. Unfortunately very little is known about him before he arrived in Constantinople. The noble Giustiniani family was found in Genoa, Venice and many other parts of Italy but its most famous members are those of Genoa, where the Giustinianis provided soldiers, clerics, writers and political leaders from the 14th century onwards.

Giovanni Giustiniani Longo was himself a professional soldier who had earlier served as *podesta* or military commander in the vital Genoese colony of Kaffa. By the time he arrived in Constantinople in January 1453 at the head of 700 troops he was considered an expert in siege warfare. Consequently, he was put in command of the city's land defences. Mortally wounded in the final Ottoman assault, Giovanni died on his way home. The Giustiniani family, however, continued to play a prominent role in Italian affairs into the 19th and 20th centuries.

Cardinal Isidore was born at Monemvasia in southern Greece around 1385, was educated in Constantinople, became a monk in the Morea, then returned to Constantinople in 1417 as *hegoumenos* or abbot of the important St Demetrios Monastery. Isidore was also a noted humanist, a friend and follower of the famous Neoplatonist scholar Georgios Gemisthos Plethon.- None of this seemed to prepare him for his warlike role in defence of Constantinople, but perhaps Isidore's open-mindedness enabled him to accept that the only real hope for Byzantium's survival lay in western Europe.

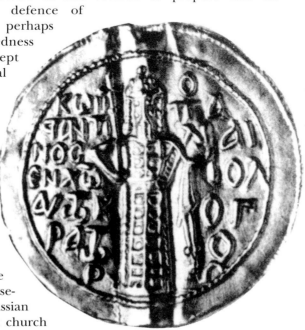

In 1434 Isidore was sent by the emperor as an Orthodox Church representative to the Council of Basle. Isidore was next sent to Russia as Metropolitan or supreme figure in the Russian Church, subsequently leading a Russian delegation to the next church

LEFT **The supposed sword of Emperor Constantine XI is a fine quality Middle Eastern sabre decorated with religious images. The Greek inscription on the other side reads: 'Christ, you, the invincible King, the Word of God, Master of all things – For the ruler and faithful autocrat Constantine.' (Armeria Reale, Turin)**

LEFT BELOW **A gold seal of Constantine XI, last Emperor of Byzantium. The tragic ruler of Constantinople appears in the full imperial regalia. (State Archives, Dubrovnik).**

council in Ferrara and Florence. Here Isidore signed the Decree of Union, but this was a step too far for the Russians, and in 1441 Isidore, by now a cardinal in the Roman Church, was imprisoned by the Russian Grand Duke Basil II. He soon escaped back to Italy and spent the rest of his life working for a union of the Latin and Orthodox churches.

It was during one of these efforts that Cardinal Isidore found himself caught up in the final siege of Constantinople, where he had been sent as a Papal Legate at the head of a small military contingent. When the city fell this remarkable churchman escaped once again, to be made Latin Patriarch of Constantinople by Pope Pius II. It was, however, a meaningless title and the unfortunate Cardinal Isidore is said to have suffered senile dementia in his final years, dying in Rome in 1463.

RIGHT **Wall painting of Manuel Hadzikis above his tomb, 15th century. This nobleman wears typical Byzantine costume, including a tall hat with an upturned brim. (*in situ* Pantanassa Church, Mistra; author's photograph)**

THE OPPOSING ARMIES

OTTOMAN ARMIES

By the mid-15th century the majority of the Ottoman professional soldiers consisted of contractual *sipahi* cavalry or *Kapi Kulu* troops of slave or prisoner-of-war origin. The former were greater in number and in some parts of mid-15th-century Rumelia at least half of the *timariots,* or fief-holding *sipahis,* were still local Christians. The *Kapi Kulu*, especially those of the sultan's own household or palace regiments, were fewer and formed an élite which was expensive both to recruit and to train. The famous Janissary infantry were simply one part of the *Kapi Kulu* palace regiments.

LEFT **The old centre of Istanbul is now so built up that few pictures can suggest its open and almost agricultural state in the mid-15th century. This view from near the Aya Sofia Mosque towards what was the Prosphorianus Harbour does, however, hint at the verdant character of medieval Constantinople. (Frederick Nicolle photograph)**

The bulk of Ottoman infantry were not Janissaries but the *Azaps* who had replaced the earlier *piyade* and *yaya* levy of Turkish foot soldiers. The *Azaps* were irregular light infantry, mostly archers with minimal training, enlisted from the Muslim peasantry and summoned for a single campaign. The majority of irregular cavalry now seem to have been *akinci* frontier light horsemen, who were similarly summoned rather than being volunteers.

At the time of Sultan Mehmet II the largely Christian *Voynuq* auxiliaries from Rumelia included Slavs and Romanian-speaking Vlachs. An élite heavily armoured Christian cavalryman was sometimes called a *lagator* and was often accompanied by a more lightly armoured *gebelü*, or squire. Ottoman forces also included Turcoman Muslim auxiliaries from Anatolia, but they do not seem to have played a significant role during the siege of Constantinople.

Even though the majority of Janissaries at the siege of Constantinople were probably recruited as prisoners-of-war, it was *Kapi Kulu* recruited through the *devsirme* system who were now coming to dominate the Ottoman army. They had been forcibly, though not always reluctantly, enlisted as boys or youths from the Christian peasant population of the Balkans, most being Slav and Albanian since Greeks tended to live on islands or in cities which were exempt from *devsirme* conscription. Not all such conscripts entered the Janissary corps as the best were creamed off for government service or the *Kapi Kulu* cavalry. Most of the palace cavalry regiments except for the *gureba* (see below) were increasingly recruited through the *devsirme*. Under Sultan Mehmet II the ranks of *timariot* provincial cavalry were also gradually filled with *Kapi Kulu* men.

The organisation and command structure of the Ottoman army was the same in peace as in war. The hierarchy of command was unambiguous and military units were permanent formations, provincial contingents under the *Beylerbeyis* of Rumelia and Anatolia being as fully under the sultan's command as his own palace regiments. As a result the Ottoman army was probably the best disciplined and trained force of its day. The classic Ottoman military structure probably existed by the time of the siege of Constantinople with the Rumelian and Anatolian provincial forces consisting of three elements: the *toprakli süvarisi* fief-holding cavalry, the *serhadkulu süvarisi* frontier cavalry and the *yerlikulu piyâdesi* local infantry. The *Beylerbeyis* of Rumelia or Anatolia were in command of local *sancak beyis*, each of whom commanded up to 50 *subasis* in an *ocak*, or regiment. The auxiliary and largely Christian *Voynuqs* were commanded by *Çeri-basi* officers under the overall command of the *Voynuq Beyi*.

The structure of the sultan's own palace or household regiments was similar, consisting of six regiments of prestigious *Kapikulu Süvarisi* cavalry, plus the *Kapikulu Piyadesi* infantry, who included the Janissaries, the *Bostancis*, the *Segmen* 'dog handlers' and *Doganci* 'falconers' from the Sultan's militarised hunting establishment, various small guard units, youngsters under training, artillery, armourers and support formations. The size of the Ottoman army was, in fact, consistently exaggerated by its foes. In reality each *sancak* (province) supported around 400 cavalry, while the Janissary corps grew from around 5,000 to 8,000 men under Mehmet II, but only after the fall of Constantinople.

Ottoman tactics were sophisticated, but during the siege of Constantinople it was their skill with artillery which brought them

RIGHT **During the 15th century a remarkable series of tombs was carved in Bosnia, perhaps reflecting the influence of the country's Bogomil (Manichaean) minority. Two panels on this tomb illustrate the light cavalry and infantry archers who formed a major part of Balkan armies. (Historical Museum, Sarajevo; author's photograph)**

BELOW RIGHT **A complete and highly decorated example of the so-called 'turban helmet' used by Ottoman sipahi cavalry, 15th–16th century (private collection).**

BELOW CENTRE **Simpler 15th–16th-century turban helmet, perhaps for an ordinary sipahi. (State Historical Museum Conservation Department, Moscow; author's photograph)**

BELOW LEFT **A simple Ottoman helmets reportedly found with the better known pieces of 15th-century Italian armour in the Castle of Halkis. (Historical Museum, Athens; Claude Blair photograph)**

success, as well as an ability to combine their efforts on land and sea. Some tactics and capabilities were, of course, applicable in both open battle and siege warfare. The supposed Serbian Janissary Konstantin Mihailovic made it clear that the initial phases of an Ottoman attack were primarily psychological, making great use of noise and military music. A particular rank of lower officers, the *çavuses*, also had an important role to play as they reported directly to the sultan, not only on the behaviour of the men but also of their officers.

Ottoman cavalry traditions and tactics had virtually nothing in common with the Turks' nomadic Central Asian past. Armoured cavalry made little use of bows and were quite as skilled fighting on foot (as they did in the siege of Constantinople) as on horseback. Less is known about infantry training in the 15th century Ottoman army, but it clearly emphasised archery in the disciplined Byzantine and Arab manner, rather than the earlier skirmishing and harassment tradition of Turks. Other evidence shows that Ottoman foot soldiers were skilled in the construction and use of siege works and, most notable of all, they were far better able to cope with reverses than were their Christian opponents.

Firearms had been spreading across the Balkans and into Ottoman territory since the 1370s. While it might be an exaggeration to say that artillery conquered Constantinople, the Ottoman army was now the most advanced in the Islamic world when it came to the use of firearms. The *Topcu* gunners corps and the *Top Arabaci* gun carriage drivers had both been created by Sultan Mehmet II's father, whereas the *Cebeci* armourers were established by Mehmet himself. All formed part of the *Kapi Kulu* palace army, and the sultan also recruited gunmakers and engineers from abroad. An illegal export of arms, including guns, continued from Italy to the Ottomans, and Anconan merchants were selling gun barrels in Constantinople a decade or so after the city fell to Sultan Mehmet. Ottoman gunfounders were not,

29

however, able to make large cast-iron cannon for many decades, their larger guns being made either of bronze or built up of iron hoops and staves. Though Ottoman cannon may have been old-fashioned, Ottoman artillerymen were at the forefront of their art and no other ruler, except Duke Philip of Burgundy, rivalled Sultan Mehmet II in promoting firearms. Mehmet's own knowledge of ballistics was ahead of his time and he was even credited with inventing a new form of long-range mortar during the siege of Constantinople.

Ottoman military engineers are said to have learned much from their Hungarian foes during the early 15th century, but in fact the heritage of Islamic siege engineering was longer and more sophisticated than that of Europe. Wooden siege towers and rams had been largely abandoned since the late 12th century as a result of the Muslims' highly developed incendiary weapons. Stone-throwing mangonels continued to be used, but these, and some briefly revived wooden siege towers, proved ineffective against the walls of Constantinople in 1453.

The Ottoman fleet was a separate arm by the mid-15th century and probably had its own dockyard and arsenal organisation. With its main base at Gallipoli, its initial role was to ensure that Ottoman armies could cross between Anatolia and Rumelia without hindrance. Nevertheless, this Ottoman fleet was virtually destroyed by the Venetians outside Gallipoli in 1416. By 1442 the Ottomans reportedly had 60 ships with a squadron based at the Byzantine vassal island of Lemnos and six years later at least 65 vessels supported a demonstration against Constantinople. Despite this, the size of the fleet that appeared outside Constantinople in 1453 came as a shock to the Byzantines and Italians alike.

ABOVE **The medieval Byzantine sea-walls still stand along the shore of what is now called Sarayburnu. The biggest dome is that of the Aya or Santa Sofia, while the small dome to the right is that of the St Irene Church. The Byzantine Old Palace ran from just left of Aya Sofia, though the trees towards the sea-walls on the far left. (Author's photograph)**

RIGHT **Another Italian artist whose work was influenced by late 15th-century Balkan costume, arms and armour was the Venetian Carpaccio. To the left are ships like those which traded with Constantinople. In the background are the sea-walls of a coastal port, while the soldiers in the foreground are typical of Venetian colonial garrisons. (St Ursula Cycle, Accademia, Venice)**

The Venetians constantly underestimated the skill and initiative of the Ottoman navy but the Ottomans had several highly developed nautical traditions to draw upon: those of Byzantium itself, the Turkish *beyliks* into which Byzantium fragmented in the 13th and 14th centuries, and the nautical practices of the Islamic Middle East. Since the Ottomans learned so much about land warfare from the Mamluks of Egypt and Syria, they probably also had access to the Mamluks' nautical

knowledge. If so, then the Ottomans made considerably more successful use of it than did the Mamluks.

The men who manned the new Ottoman navy were clearly not all Muslims and not all Turks. There was still a substantial Greek population in Gallipoli, only part of which seems to have converted to Islam, while other non-Muslims in Gallipoli may have included Italians and Catalans, or at least the descendants of such settlers. Ottoman ships were essentially the same as those of other Mediterranean fleets, a very common fighting vessel being a fast, light and manoeuvrable galley with a boarding beak and stern rudder. The Ottoman *mavna* was a larger vessel like the Italian *galeazza* or Great Galley, but this may not have appeared in any numbers until later in the 15th century.

CHRISTIAN FORCES

The overall population of Constantinople, excluding Galata, was probably now between 40,000 and 50,000 people, with a regular garrison of a few hundred. A list of defenders made for the emperor by the government official Sphrantzes gave a total of 4,973 Greeks, both professional soldiers and militiamen, plus 200 resident foreigners. The number of foreigners is, however, clearly misleading as it only included

BELOW LEFT 'Iskender attacking a fortress in Sistan'. Crudely drawn cannon are used by both besiegers and defenders in this picture from the late 15th-century Ottoman *Iskendername*. Once again Iskender (Alexander) carries a European-style shield. (Institute of Oriental Studies, Ms. C. 133, f.52b, St Petersburg)

BELOW RIGHT Another miniature painting in the late 15th-century Ottoman *Iskendername* shows a battle between the cavalry of Alexander the Great and the King of Kashmir. On the right Iskender carries what is clearly a European shield with a double-headed imperial eagle. Otherwise he and the other horsemen have Turco-Persian arms and armour. (Institute of Oriental Studies, Ms. C. 133, f.119b, St Petersburg)

ABOVE **The superb carvings on the Triumphal Arch of Alfonso V of Aragon in Naples, made between 1455 and 1458 by Francesco Laurana, illustrate the sort of arms and armour that would have been used by many of the defenders of Constantinople, Italians and Byzantine. (***in situ* Castel Nuovo, Naples)**

permanent residents. Most estimates of the number of men who defended the walls in 1453 range from 6,000 to 8,500, most of whom were barely trained local militias. However, Archbishop Leonard of Chios, who took part in the siege, puts the number of active defenders at around 6,000 Greeks and 3,000 foreigners. Giacomo Tedaldi was also there and subsequently wrote a concise report for the Cardinal of Avignon in January 1454. It is perhaps the calmest and most objective account of all, reporting that: 'In the city there were altogether 30,000 to 35,000 men under arms and six to seven thousand real soldiers, making 42,000 at the most.'

By the 15th century the remnants of the Byzantine Empire were too poor to hire many mercenaries. Defence therefore fell to local troops, local militias and foreign volunteers including European soldiers and sailors who, for whatever reason, found themselves at the emperor's gate. The soldiers who accompanied Emperor John VIII to Italy in 1437 included two distinct types of cavalry: armoured *stradioti*, who would probably have rated as light cavalry in western Europe, and even more lightly equipped *gianitzaroi*. Powerful Byzantine noblemen also had their own military followings and Byzantine soldiers who held land as *pronoia* fiefs were not militarised peasants but still formed a local élite. Many of them, particularly within the *Despotate* of the Morea, which was the only substantial bloc of territory still in Byzantine hands, were of

33

non-Greek origin including Slavs, Albanians and descendants of Latin Crusader or Italian colonial feudal élites.

In the 15th century Constantinople consisted of separated village-sized settlements within the vast ancient walls; there was a more substantial urban area at the easternmost end, parts of which were allocated to foreign merchants such as the Venetians. This probably provided a framework for a structured militia within each quarter or 'urban village' organised under a *demarchos* and supervised by imperial officials. Since Greek monasteries in rural areas employed armed guards, and monks did duty in their monastery's *vigla* observation towers, references to monks patrolling the ramparts of Constantinople should not come as much of a surprise. Constantinople also had a substantial Turkish Muslim population by this time, though whether any of them chose to support the Ottoman pretender, Prince Orhan, in the final siege is unclear.

Otherwise the military organisation of the remaining Byzantine forces is very unclear. The little army in Constantinople itself may still have been known as the *politicon* army, but whether it was still divided into *allagia* (regiments) is unknown. Infantry archers and crossbowmen certainly played a major role. In fact Byzantine crossbowmen were something of an élite, forming themselves into 'brotherhoods' rather like those seen in medieval Italy.

Written sources are clearer when it comes to descriptions of Byzantine troops. They wore western European-style armour, probably of western origin. The defenders of Constantinople clearly had firearms, but they were considerably smaller than the Ottoman 'great guns'. Most came from Italy, Hungary or the Balkans along with a larger number of smaller handguns. In 1453 the Byzantines also use 'Greek Fire' under supervision of Johannes Grant, who is believed to have been a Scot who arrived in Constantinople via Germany.

The massive land-walls of Constantinople had been improved since they were built centuries earlier, but their essential layout remained the same. The biggest change was at the northern end where the 12th-century Emperor Manuel had enclosed the Blachernae Palace with a single, more modern wall and towers, but without a deep moat. A low wall or breastwork had been erected along the inside of the moat in 1341 and this seems to have been strengthened or modernised between 1433 and 1448 in a final attempt to repel the Ottoman threat. The last improvements to the walls also reflected the new threat from cannon though even in Constantinople's most exposed defences there was a notable lack of emplacements for defensive firearms. Another major defensive feature was the floating chain or boom supported by massive wooden floáts which

ABOVE **The Garamszentbenedeki Altar was painted by Koloszvári Tamas in 1427. The Crucifixion scene includes a clear representation of Hungarian arms and armour of the mid-15th century. Although it was similar to the military equipment of Germany, it tended to be more old-fashioned, and the same was true of Serbian and Wallachian equipment. (Kereszteny Museum, Esztergom)**

RIGHT **The soldier to the right of the Resurrection scene from the Garamszentbenedeki Altar holds a small Lithuanian pavise-style shield, a characteristically eastern European piece of equipment. (Kereszteny Museum, Esztergom)**

ran from a tower below Acropolis Point to the sea-wall of Galata, thus closing the Golden Horn. Because the walls of Constantinople enclosed so much open space, the city's reduced population could grow quite a lot of its own food, while abundant fish could be caught in the waters outside. There was even space to graze animals.

Most of the remaining Byzantine coastal towns in Thrace were abandoned without a fight when the Ottomans advanced in 1453, though some put up a fierce resistance. The reasons for this are not known, but it may be significant that Therapia was on the Bosphorus, north of the Ottoman blockade at Rumeli Hisar, while Selymbria and Epibatos were behind the Ottoman siege lines on the Marmara coast. Perhaps they were intended to provide outlets to the outside world while Constantinople was besieged. The lack of a proper navy was, however, a fatal handicap for the defenders of Constantinople, the last real Byzantine fleet having been destroyed by the Genoese in the 14th century.

Western Europeans helped defend Constantinople, manning the walls and fighting as sailors or marines. In many cases these were one and the same people, though the great majority of them came from Italy. A population explosion in many Italian cities had led to an excess of young men, unemployed, unable to marry, available for adventure and often from the better-off families. In addition to the professional soldier Giovanni Giustiniani Longo, the Venetian *baillie* Girolomo Minotto and the captain of the Venetian trading fleet at Tana, Alvise Diedo, there were members from the Venetian Dolfin, Gritti, Loredano, Cornaro, Mocenigo, Trevisan and Venier families. Then there were the Genoese Girolomo and Lionardo di Langasco, Maurizio Cattaneo, the Bocchiardi brothers and others, while the Catalans were led by Père Julia. But the bulk of those who served under these men remain unnamed. In fact everyone aboard an Italian ship in eastern waters was expected to be armed, the only exceptions being clergy and pilgrims. The Italian ships that got caught up in the siege ranged from lumbering merchant vessels dependent upon sail alone, through merchant galleys using oars and sails, to lighter war-galleys.

The Dardanelles, looking from Çanakkale to the Gallipoli Peninsula. In the mid-15th century both banks were firmly under Ottoman control but the waterway itself, unlike the Bosphorus to the north, was too wide to be closed by the guns available to Sultan Mehmet II. (Author's photograph)

THE OPPOSING PLANS

THE OTTOMAN PLAN

Sultan Mehmet II's plans for the conquest of Constantinople depended upon diplomatic as much as military considerations. Above all, he had to strike quickly before western European powers like Venice and Hungary could react. On the other hand, the sultan also intended to be patient, expending gunpowder and money rather than blood. Finally, he would use new technology including heavy artillery to breach the massive walls of Constantinople, and the newly powerful Ottoman fleet to deny the city food, military supplies and moral encouragement from the outside world. At the same time Sultan Mehmet II wanted to take Constantinople with as little damage as possible and with minimal loss of life to his future Greek subjects. His generally anti-Latin policy reflected the importance he attached to winning over the Orthodox Christian Church.

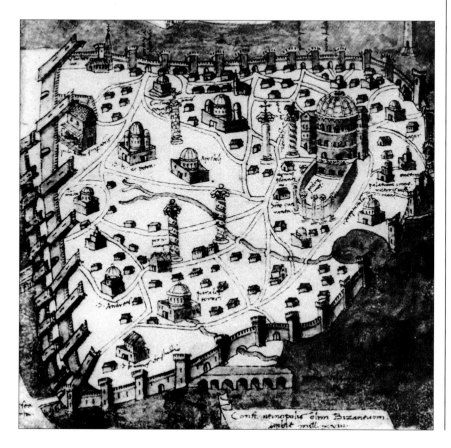

One of the earliest maps of Byzantine Constantinople appeared in the *Liber Insularium* by Cristofori Buondelmonti in 1422. Though schematic, it is remarkably accurate. The Golden Horn is at the top, the doubled land-walls with a moat on the left. The map even hints at the empty character of the land within the walls, except around the great church of Santa Sofia. (Vatican Library, Cod. Rossianus 702, f.32v, Rome)

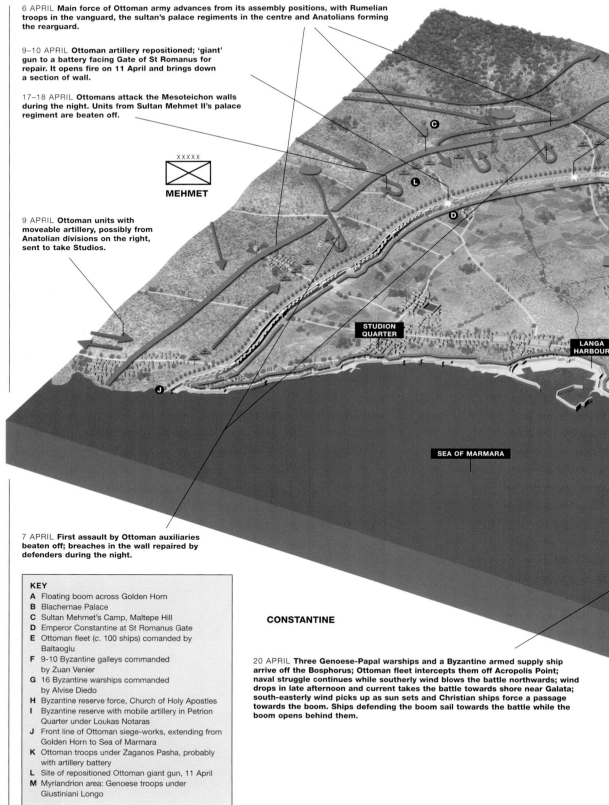

6 APRIL Main force of Ottoman army advances from its assembly positions, with Rumelian troops in the vanguard, the sultan's palace regiments in the centre and Anatolians forming the rearguard.

9–10 APRIL Ottoman artillery repositioned; 'giant' gun to a battery facing Gate of St Romanus for repair. It opens fire on 11 April and brings down a section of wall.

17–18 APRIL Ottomans attack the Mesoteichon walls during the night. Units from Sultan Mehmet II's palace regiment are beaten off.

XXXXX

MEHMET

9 APRIL Ottoman units with moveable artillery, possibly from Anatolian divisions on the right, sent to take Studios.

7 APRIL First assault by Ottoman auxiliaries beaten off; breaches in the wall repaired by defenders during the night.

STUDION QUARTER

LANGA HARBOUR

SEA OF MARMARA

KEY
A Floating boom across Golden Horn
B Blachernae Palace
C Sultan Mehmet's Camp, Maltepe Hill
D Emperor Constantine at St Romanus Gate
E Ottoman fleet (*c.* 100 ships) comanded by Baltaoglu
F 9-10 Byzantine galleys commanded by Zuan Venier
G 16 Byzantine warships commanded by Alvise Diedo
H Byzantine reserve force, Church of Holy Apostles
I Byzantine reserve with mobile artillery in Petrion Quarter under Loukas Notaras
J Front line of Ottoman siege-works, extending from Golden Horn to Sea of Marmara
K Ottoman troops under Zaganos Pasha, probably with artillery battery
L Site of repositioned Ottoman giant gun, 11 April
M Myriandrion area: Genoese troops under Giustiniani Longo

CONSTANTINE

20 APRIL Three Genoese-Papal warships and a Byzantine armed supply ship arrive off the Bosphorus; Ottoman fleet intercepts them off Acropolis Point; naval struggle continues while southerly wind blows the battle northwards; wind drops in late afternoon and current takes the battle towards shore near Galata; south-easterly wind picks up as sun sets and Christian ships force a passage towards the boom. Ships defending the boom sail towards the battle while the boom opens behind them.

THE FIRST PHASE OF THE SIEGE 2–20 APRIL, 1453

Constantinople prepared to defend itself against the forces of Sultan Mehmet, hoping that the city could hold out until the arrival of reinforcements from western Europe

6–7 APRIL Ottoman artillery bombardment breaches wall near Gate of Charisius.

■
ZAGANOS PASHA

9 APRIL First unsuccessful attack on the boom by Ottoman fleet; repeated, again without success on 12 April.

9 APRIL Ottoman units with movable artillery, possibly from Zaganos Pasha's division behind Galata, sent to take Therapia.

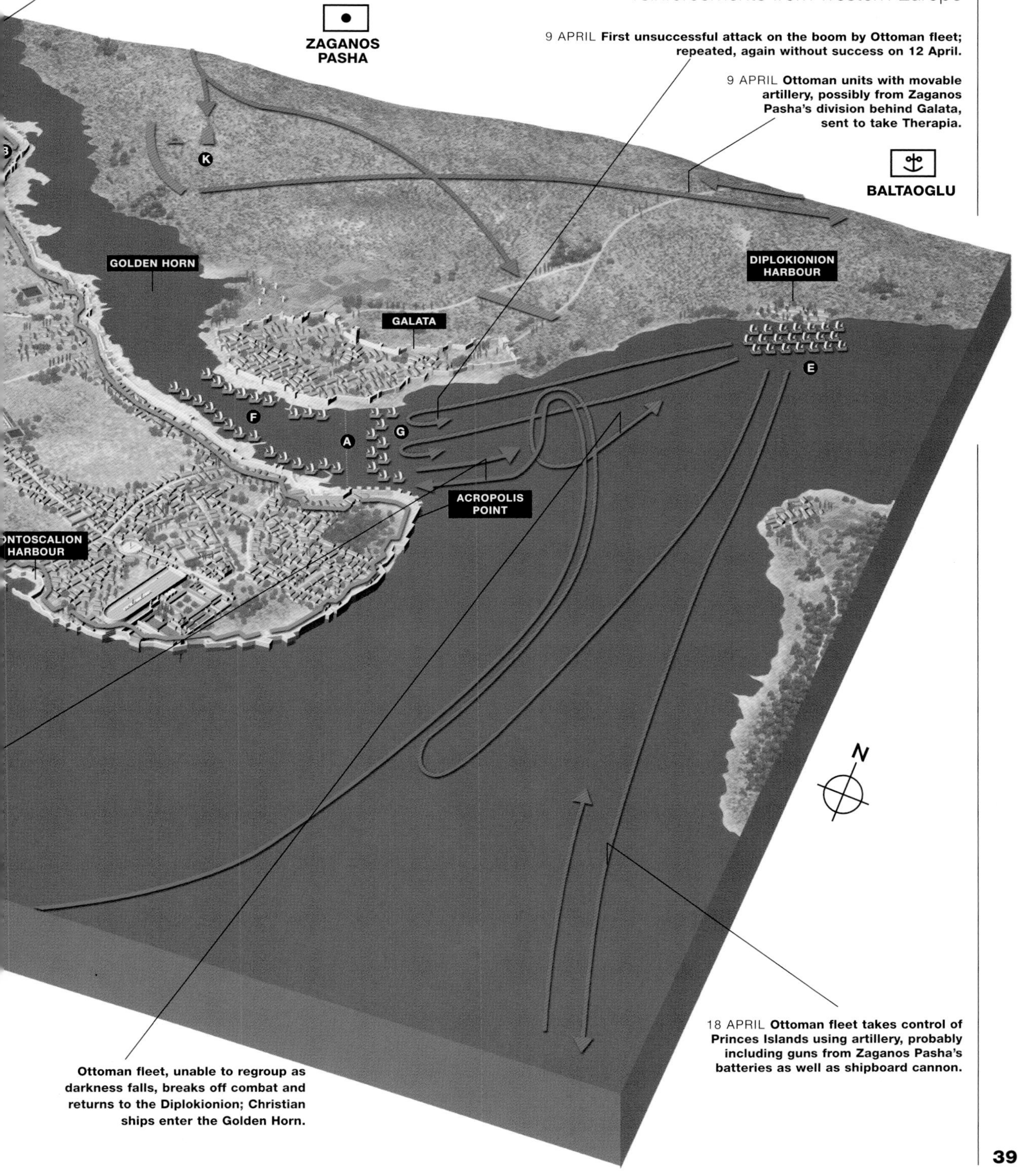

⚓
BALTAOGLU

K

GOLDEN HORN

GALATA

DIPLOKIONION HARBOUR

F

A **G**

E

ACROPOLIS POINT

NTOSCALION HARBOUR

N

18 APRIL Ottoman fleet takes control of Princes Islands using artillery, probably including guns from Zaganos Pasha's batteries as well as shipboard cannon.

Ottoman fleet, unable to regroup as darkness falls, breaks off combat and returns to the Diplokionion; Christian ships enter the Golden Horn.

THE BYZANTINE PLAN

The Emperor Constantine XI's plans were the exact opposite of those of Sultan Mehmet. He and his advisers knew that the outcome would depend on the time factor. If the defenders could endure long enough, help would eventually come from outside, if not as a Hungarian invasion, then by sea from Italy. Constantine was absolutely correct, but unfortunately for the remnants of the Byzantine Empire, the Ottomans' cannon intensified the siege, and the Ottoman fleet brought the attack to bear on every side of Constantinople, even the Golden Horn.

More immediately, Giustiniani Longo believed that the outermost rampart of Constantinople's land-walls should be defended. This tactic had succeeded in 1422 and would, he thought, make the best use of the city's outnumbered defenders while the high inner walls were manned by archers, crossbowmen and gunners. In fact Constantinople's walls were still so strong that, even in the context of mid-15th century warfare, the Ottoman numerical advantage at first had little impact. Even though the Byzantines and Italians did not expect such aggressive action from the Ottoman fleet, there was little danger of the walls along the Marmara coast being breached, and with adequate ships in the Golden Horn the defenders felt confident of protecting the floating boom. Again they were correct – until the Ottomans seized the Golden Horn behind them. Clearly the idea that Constantinople was inevitably doomed is wrong, and the overall situation was not as one-sided as a simple glance at a map might suggest.

ABOVE **The interior of one of the few relatively accessible original chambers in a tower of the inner wall. These structures were, however, frequently repaired and in many cases modernised during their long history. (Author's photograph)**

LEFT **This section of Constantinople's land-walls is at a high point before the land dips towards the Golden Horn, just north of what was the Gate of Charisius. The outer breastwork and fosse have entirely disappeared. (Author's photograph)**

THE CAMPAIGN

CLOSING THE NOOSE

'Khusrau hunting' in a copy of *Khusrau wa Shirin* by Hatifi, Ottoman c.1498. Ottoman painting was vigorous, colourful and full of realistic details. Note the mounted Janissary picking up a bird on the right of this picture. (Metropolitan Museum, Harris Brisbane Dick Fund, 1969, 62, 27, New York)

In January 1453 Sultan Mehmet II returned to Edirne, where large numbers of volunteers were mustering for the campaign. In addition to the Rumelian and palace contingents the troops were augmented by camp-followers including merchants to supply Ottoman troops with food and necessities. Early in 1453 a Serbian vassal contingent also arrived, reportedly consisting of 1,500 Christian cavalry and auxiliaries under the *voivode* of Jaksa; Serbian miners arrived from Novo Brdo considerably later. According to the Italian Giacomo Tedaldi, Christians in the Ottoman ranks were allowed to worship as they wished.

Karaca, the *Beylerbeyi* of Rumelia, sent men to prepare the roads from Edirne to Constantinople so that the bridges could cope with massive cannon. Fifty carpenters and 200 assistants also strengthened the roads where necessary. There was no reported resistance and Karaca Bey's pioneers went on to cut down vines and orchards outside the walls of Constantinople to provide a clear field of fire for the Ottoman artillery. In February Karaca Bey's troops also began to take the remaining Byzantine towns along the Marmara and Black Sea coasts. Again, there was minimal resistance and consequently no removal of the Christian population. Only those places which defied the Ottomans were sacked. Silivri, Epibatos and Therapia opposed the invaders and were therefore bypassed, although some troops probably stayed to observe them. Bursa was the main assembly area for Anatolian units and three regiments crossed the Bosphorus to help the Rumelians watch Constantinople. During March larger numbers of *azaps* and *sipahis* crossed via Rumeli Hisar, followed by their commander, Ishak Pasha the *Beylerbeyi* of Anatolia.

Next, the Ottomans brought their massive guns to the walls of Constantinople, the biggest of the three 'giant' guns requiring 60 oxen to pull it. The artillery then assembled 5 miles (8 km) from the walls, guarded by Karaca Bey's troops. Meanwhile, the Ottoman fleet under Baltaoglu had gathered outside Gallipoli. In March it sailed for Constantinople and established a base at Diplokionion Bay on the Bosphorus just north of Galata.

The Byzantines still had access to the sea and during the winter of 1452–53 their remaining galleys raided Turkish villages as far as the

THE OTTOMAN ADVANCE ON CONSTANTINOPLE, JANUARY–MARCH 1453

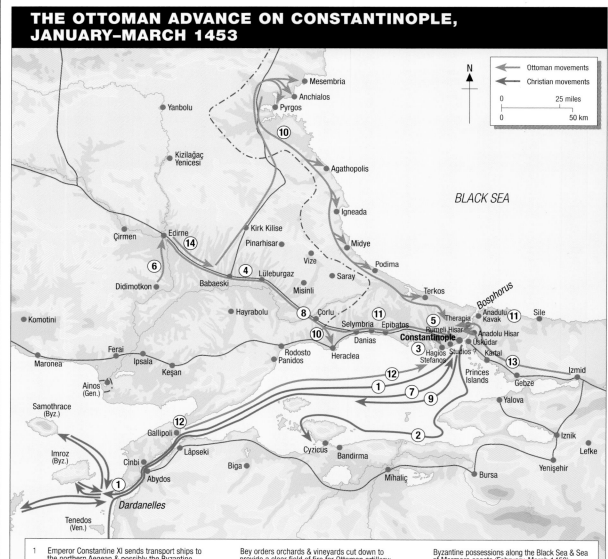

1. Emperor Constantine XI sends transport ships to the northern Aegean & possibly the Byzantine Morea to purchase food & military equipment (winter 1452-53).
2. Byzantine galleys raid Ottoman coastal villages as far as Cyzicus (winter 1452-53).
3. Emperor Constantine XI orders silver in churches & monasteries to be melted for coin to pay troops; final improvements to the fortifications of Constantinople (winter 1452-53).
4. *Beylerbeyi* Karaca Bey of Rumelia has the road from Edirne repaired & strengthened for heavy cannon (winter 1452-53).
5. Ottoman units from Anatolia cross the Bosphorus via Rumeli Hisar to watch Constantinople; Karaca

Bey orders orchards & vineyards cut down to provide a clear field of fire for Ottoman artillery; construction of siege lines begins (winter 1452-53).
6. Mehmet II returns from Didimotkon & spends the winter planning the siege of Constantinople.
7. Giovanni Giustiniani Longo with Genoese galleys & 700 soldiers arrives in Constantinople where Emperor Constantine XI makes him commander of the land defences (26 or 29 January 1453).
8. Ottoman advance guard under Karaca Bey brings the artillery from Edirne (February 1453).
9. Venetian ship commanded by Pietro Davanzo and six Cretan merchant ships leave the Golden Horn without permission (26 February 1453).
10. Other Rumelian contingents capture remaining

Byzantine possessions along the Black Sea & Sea of Marmara coasts (February-March 1453).
11. Selymbria, Epibatos & Studios (probable position) on the Marmara coast, & Therapia on the Bosphorus, resist Karaca Bey's forces & remain in Byzantine hands.
12. Ottoman fleet, already assembled at Gallipoli, sails to the Bosphorus to help transfer of Anatolian troops (March 1453).
13. Ottoman Anatolian contingents under *Beylerbeyi* Ishak Pasha of Anatolia, cross the Bosphorus (March 1453).
14. Sultan Mehmet II leaves Edirne with his Palace Regiments (23 March 1453).

THE OTTOMAN BLOCKADE AND SIEGE OF CONSTANTINOPLE, 2 APRIL–29 MAY 1453

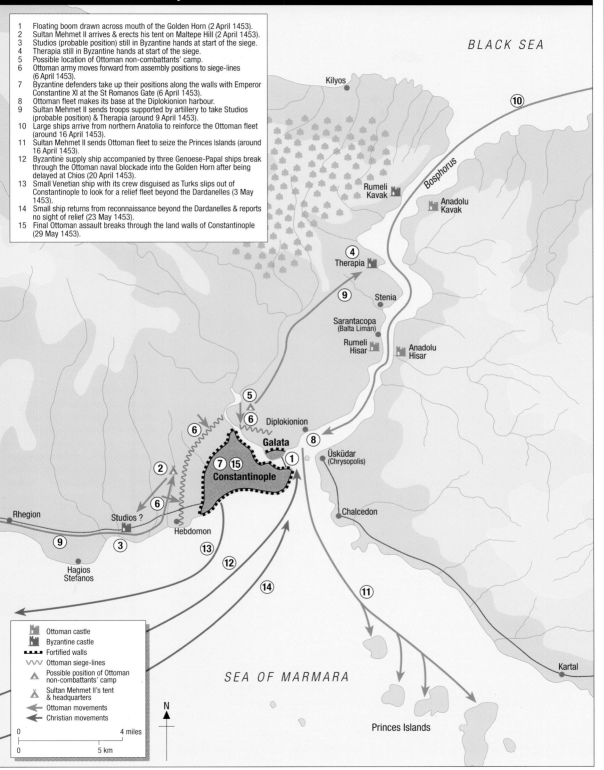

1   Floating boom drawn across mouth of the Golden Horn (2 April 1453).
2   Sultan Mehmet II arrives & erects his tent on Maltepe Hill (2 April 1453).
3   Studios (probable position) still in Byzantine hands at start of the siege.
4   Therapia still in Byzantine hands at start of the siege.
5   Possible location of Ottoman non-combattants' camp.
6   Ottoman army moves forward from assembly positions to siege-lines (6 April 1453).
7   Byzantine defenders take up their positions along the walls with Emperor Constantine XI at the St Romanos Gate (6 April 1453).
8   Ottoman fleet makes its base at the Diplokionion harbour.
9   Sultan Mehmet II sends troops supported by artillery to take Studios (probable position) & Therapia (around 9 April 1453).
10 Large ships arrive from northern Anatolia to reinforce the Ottoman fleet (around 16 April 1453).
11 Sultan Mehmet II sends Ottoman fleet to seize the Princes Islands (around 16 April 1453).
12 Byzantine supply ship accompanied by three Genoese-Papal ships break through the Ottoman naval blockade into the Golden Horn after being delayed at Chios (20 April 1453).
13 Small Venetian ship with its crew disguised as Turks slips out of Constantinople to look for a relief fleet beyond the Dardanelles (3 May 1453).
14 Small ship returns from reconnaissance beyond the Dardanelles & reports no sight of relief (23 May 1453).
15 Final Ottoman assault breaks through the land walls of Constantinople (29 May 1453).

BLACK SEA

Kilyos

Bosphorus

Rumeli Kavak

Anadolu Kavak

Therapia

Stenia

Sarantacopa (Balta Liman)

Rumeli Hisar

Anadolu Hisar

Diplokionion

Galata

Constantinople

Üsküdar (Chrysopolis)

Rhegion

Studios ?

Hebdomon

Chalcedon

Hagios Stefanos

SEA OF MARMARA

Kartal

Princes Islands

Legend

- Ottoman castle
- Byzantine castle
- Fortified walls
- Ottoman siege-lines
- Possible position of Ottoman non-combattants' camp
- Sultan Mehmet II's tent & headquarters
- Ottoman movements
- Christian movements

N

0   4 miles
0   5 km

Cyzikos peninsula on the southern side of the Sea of Marmara. On 26 February Pietro Davanzo's ship slipped out, followed by six Cretan vessels with 700 people aboard. They reached Tenedos safely, but the arrival of the Ottoman fleet off Constantinople in March meant that future ships maintaining communication with the outside world had to slip out quietly at night.

Most of the Ottoman ships were newly built, but some were old and had needed repair; estimates of the size of Baltaoglu's fleet vary wildly. According to the Ottoman *Asiqpasazade* there were 400 of all sizes. Kritovoulos put the Ottoman fleet at 350 ships plus transports. A remarkably specific report by Jehan de Wavrin, probably taken from an official Burgundian document, states that there were 18 war-galleys, 60 to 70 smaller *galliots*, and 16 to 20 small craft, while Giacomo Tedaldi specifies that these were 16 to 20 horse-transports. Another realistic report puts the total at six large galleys, ten ordinary galleys, 15 small galleys or *galiots*, 75 *fustae* (which were hardly more than large rowing boats), 20 horse-transports and numerous small boats.

The Byzantines were now confined within the walls of Constantinople, and the Greek courtier Sphrantzes described how the emperor sought to maximise the city's defences: 'The Emperor ordered the tribunes to take a census of their communities and record the exact numbers of men, laity and clergy, able to defend the walls and what weapons each man had for the defence. All tribunes completed this task and brought the lists of their communities to the Emperor. The Emperor said to me, "The task is for you and no one else, as you are skilled in arithmetic, and also know how

ABOVE **'Battle between Byzantines and Turks'** on the so-called Trebizond Cassone, made in Florence in the mid-15th century. The two sides are almost identical except for the tall caps and flat-topped heraldic shields of the Byzantines. (Metropolitan Museum, New York)

ABOVE RIGHT **'Iskender slays a Dragon'** in the late 15th century *Iskendername*. Iskender, wearing characteristic Ottoman costume and riding in a covered wagon, strikes with a curved sabre. (Institute of Oriental Studies, Ms. C.133, f.93b, St Petersburg)

BELOW RIGHT **An isolated tower and the ruined defences of Vize,** a small town to the west of Istanbul. Its fortifications would have been typical of those Thracian towns remaining in Byzantine hands at the start of the 15th century. (Author's photograph)

to guard and keep secrets."' The result was, however, so low that Constantine told Sphrantzes to keep it quiet.

Archbishop Leonard of Chios added that: 'The greater part of the Greeks were men of peace, using their shields and spears, their bows and swords, according to the light of nature rather than with any skill. The majority had helmets and body armour of metal or leather, and fought with swords and spears. Those who were skilled in the use of the bow or the crossbow were not enough to man all the ramparts.' Around 1,000 Byzantine troops were also kept back as a reserve within the city.

The defenders' position appeared better in naval terms, and the assorted vessels in the Golden Horn expected to hold their own, including powerful Italian ships with experienced crews which had sought refuge in Constantinople on their way home from the Black Sea. Twenty-six could be rated as fighting ships: five from Genoa, five from Venice, three from Venetian Crete, one each from Ancona, Spain and France, and about ten Byzantines.

OTTOMAN ARTILLERYMEN PUT A HUGE CANNON INTO POSITION BEFORE THE START OF THE SIEGE, SUPERVISED BY URBAN THE HUNGARIAN GUN MASTER (MARCH 1453).

Ottoman artillery at the siege of Constantinople was essentially the same as that seen elsewhere in Europe, and Urban's biggest cannon was probably built up of wrought iron staves and hoops. In the 15th century large guns were placed in sloping trenches with massive wooden blocks as shock absorbers. Altering the aim of such weapons was slow and difficult. Ottoman 'giant' guns also formed part of batteries which included smaller cannon. Between these and the walls of Constantinople lay the Ottoman front line consisting of a trench with an earth embankment topped by a wooden palisade.

On 2 April 1453 the floating chain or boom was drawn across the Golden Horn, supervised by the Genoese engineer Bartolomeo Soligo. The Genoese authorities in Galata decided to remain neutral, but some men and ships slipped across the Golden Horn to help defend Constantinople. The Venetians who lived in the city had no choice but to fight under the command of the Venetian *baillie*, Girolomo Minotto. In fact Emperor Constantine XI asked Minotto's men to parade their banners along the wall to show the Ottomans they would soon be fighting Venetians. The keys of four vital gates were similarly entrusted to the Venetians, while defence of the emperor's own Blachernae Palace was entrusted to the *baillie*. Filippo Contarini commanded the wall between the Pege and Golden gates, Jacopo Contarini the Studion quarter, and Venetian and Genoese sailors under Gabriele Trevisan much of the walls along the Golden Horn. Alvise Diedo commanded ships in the Golden Horn, while those protecting the boom were under Zuan Venier. Giustiniani Longo commanded at many as 2,000 Greeks and Italians on the central section of the land-walls which was correctly seen as the most threatened sector.

A hurried attempt to excavate a fosse around the exposed Blachernae walls was left to men from the Venetian great galley from Tana, among others. But the bales of wool and leather sheets hung outside the walls to absorb the shock of cannonballs proved useless against Sultan Mehmet's modern artillery. Each tower from the Golden to Horaia gates was manned by an archer supported by a crossbowman or a hand-gunner, and Loukas Notaras placed some mobile cannon as a reserve in the Petrion quarter.

ABOVE **A relief carving of a mounted warrior saint over the door of a Serbian monastery church, 14th-15th century. It shows a man with ordinary European light cavalry equipment, apparently including the massive rigid bevor to protect his neck which also appears in paintings of this period. (*in situ* west door of the Narthex of Radoslav, Church of Joachim and Anne, Monastery of Studenica; author's photograph)**

ABOVE **The road from Edirne to Constantinople (Istanbul) ran along the Marmara coast after reaching the shore west of Selymbria (Silivri). It then had to cross two inlets which cut deep inland: this one at Büyükçekmece, and a second at Küç Çekmece. Another inland route via Vize was probably unsuitable for the Ottoman army's great cannon. (Author's photograph)**

LEFT **The painted front of the Trebizond Cassone, made in 15th-century Florence also includes a stylised representation of Constantinople with a number of ships in the Golden Horn, shown here on the right. (Metropolitan Museum, New York)**

Sultan Mehmet and the main Ottoman force left Edirne on 23 March 1453 and assembled about 2 miles (4 km) from Constantinople. A later source maintains that the main Ottoman encampment was on the other side of the Golden Horn, this perhaps being the site of the pioneers', labourers' and non-combatants' camp. The artillery was already in position close to the walls in 14 or 15 batteries spread along the land-walls. Three such batteries faced Blachernae and included one of Urban's giant guns, probably the second largest named *Basiliske*. Two batteries faced the Gate of Charisus, four the St Romanus Gate, three the Pege Gate, with two otherwise unaccounted batteries perhaps facing the Golden Gate. Additional batteries of smaller cannon were alongside or between those of the big guns since there are said to have been a total of 69 Ottoman cannon in 15 batteries: five of four small guns, nine of four small guns plus one large, and one of four large guns facing the St Romanus Gate. The largest gun fired a ball reportedly weighing about 1,212 lb (550 kg), the second largest over 793 lb (360 kg), the others from 507 – 198 lb (230 – 90 kg). They were supported by a dozen or so sturdy stone-throwing trebuchets which had almost certainly been erected by 11 April.

Back in Europe, in late March or early April, the Pope finally sent three large Genoese ships full of arms and provisions, but they were soon storm-bound at Chios. The Venetians reacted even more slowly and it was not until 11 May that Loredan set out for Constantinople. A few days later news that the siege was under way caused near panic and three more warships were ordered to join Loredan at Tenedos. During the siege of Constantinople János Hunyadi, the Captain-General of Hungary, reportedly proposed a seaborne campaign to outflank the Ottomans, but this came to nothing.

THE SIEGE BEGINS

On 2 April, the day the boom was drawn across the Golden Horn, Sultan Mehmet II's entourage established their tents on Maltepe Hill facing the St Romanus Gate. On the 6th the bulk of the Ottoman army moved forward from its assembly positions, paused for prayers about a mile (1.5 km) from Constantinople, then moved up to the siege lines. The Rumelians were now on the left, the sultan in the centre and the Anatolians the right. Part of the army was kept in reserve, perhaps including much of the palace regiments with the auxiliaries or volunteers. Zaganos Pasha and Karaca Bey also took a few thousand men to occupy the other side of the Golden Horn, while a small unit under Kasim Pasha was sent to watch Galata.

Archbishop Leonard stated that as the Ottoman army moved forward, its troops carried 'pieces of lattice-work made out of branches

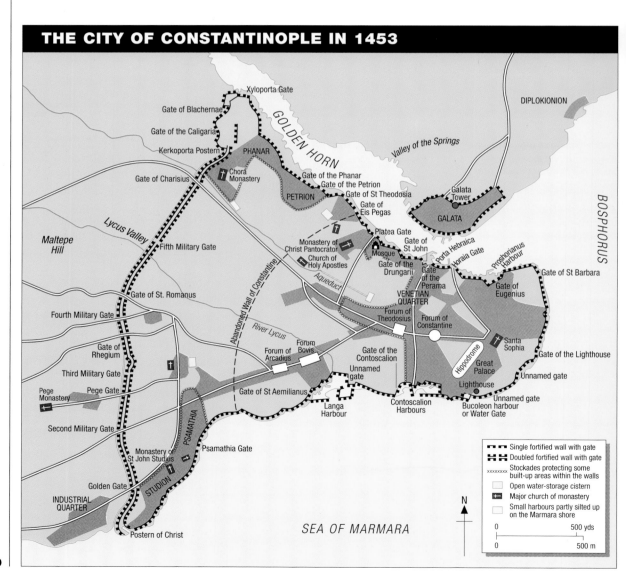

THE CITY OF CONSTANTINOPLE IN 1453

(map)

Xyloporta Gate
Gate of Blachernae
Gate of the Caligaria
Kerkoporta Postern
Gate of Charisius
PHANAR
Chora Monastery
GOLDEN HORN
Valley of the Springs
DIPLOKIONION
Gate of the Phanar
Gate of the Petrion
PETRION
Gate of St Theodosia
Gate of Eis Pegas
Galata Tower
GALATA
BOSPHORUS
Maltepe Hill
Lycus Valley
Fifth Military Gate
Monastery of Christ Pantocrator
Church of Holy Apostles
Mosque
Platea Gate
Gate of St John
Gate of the Drungarii
Porta Hebraica
Horaia Gate
Proshorianus Harbour
Gate of St Barbara
Aqueduct
Gate of the Perama
VENETIAN QUARTER
Gate of Eugenius
Gate of St. Romanus
Abandoned Wall of Constantine
Forum of Theodosius
Forum of Constantine
Fourth Military Gate
River Lycus
Forum of Arcadius
Forum Bovis
Gate of the Contoscalion
Santa Sophia
Gate of the Lighthouse
Gate of Rhegium
Hippodrome
Great Palace
Unnamed gate
Third Military Gate
Unnamed gate
Pege Monastery
Pege Gate
Gate of St Aemilianus
Langa Harbour
Contoscalion Harbours
Lighthouse
Unnamed gate
Bucoleon harbour or Water Gate
Second Military Gate
PSAMATHIA
Monastery of St John Studius
Psamathia Gate
Golden Gate
STUDION
INDUSTRIAL QUARTER
Postern of Christ
SEA OF MARMARA

Legend:
- Single fortified wall with gate
- Doubled fortified wall with gate
- xxxxxxxx Stockades protecting some built-up areas within the walls
- Open water-storage cistern
- Major church of monastery
- Small harbours partly silted up on the Marmara shore

0   500 yds
0   500 m

N

and slips of trees to protect his soldiers.' He also maintained that they could have been attacked at this point, before they occupied their siege fortifications. The fortifications were over 2 miles (4 km) long, stretching from the Marmara coast to the Golden Horn, and consisting of a trench fronted by an earth rampart, with a wooden palisade with posterns and wooden turrets. The two sides were now so close that the Turks mocked the Greeks' long beards, threatening to make them into dog-leashes.

The size of the Ottoman army facing Constantinople has been wildly exaggerated and can have included at most 80,000 fighting soldiers. The majority were cavalry, although they now fought on foot. Again Giacomo Tedaldi may be closest to the truth. 'At the siege,' he wrote, 'were altogether 200,000 men of whom perhaps 60,000 were soldiers (the rest being labourers or non-combatants), 30 to 40,000 of them cavalry.'

On the morning of 6 April Emperor Constantine XI joined Giustiniani Longo at the St Romanus Gate. The Ottoman artillery bombardment also began that day and was continued on the 7th, bringing down part of a

wall near the Gate of Charisius. On the second day Urban's big gun facing Blachernae started to overheat. This was temporarily solved by sponging the interior with oil after every shot, but on 11 April the gun either cracked or started to leak. A more widespread problem for the Ottoman artillerymen, however, was the slippage of their guns in the April mud.

The first Ottoman assault was probably launched on 7 April against the centre of the land-walls. Ill-equipped irregulars and volunteers advanced with great enthusiasm, supported by archers and hand-gunners, but were met by the defenders at the outermost rampart and were driven back with relative ease. The

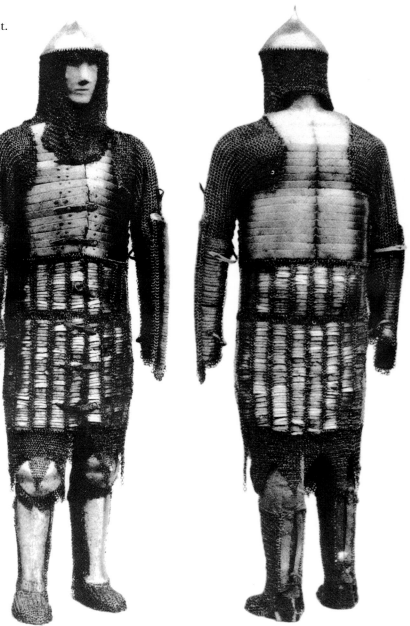

Front and rear views of a 15th-century Ottoman infantry armour. It is largely of mail-and-plate construction, with a low pointed helmet and plated greaves. (Metropolitan Museum, New York)

damaged sections of wall were also repaired the following night. Meanwhile, Byzantine guns commanded by the Bocchiardi brothers were notably effective, until the largest cannon burst. Thereafter the Byzantine cannon were largely limited to the anti-personnel role, each gun shooting from five to ten walnut-sized bullets.

During the first days of the siege the defenders made several sorties but Giustiniani decided they were losing more than they gained and so withdrew his men from the outer rampart to the first main wall. There was now a short pause during which Sultan Mehmet ordered several artillery batteries to be repositioned. On 11 or 12 April the Ottomans reopened their artillery bombardment, after which it remained almost continuous, despite problems with the elevation and aiming of the Ottoman guns. A Hungarian ambassador arrived in the Ottoman camp as an observer around this time, and according to Doukas, advised the Ottoman

These carved figures are above the door of a late medieval house in what was Venetian-ruled Dalmatia. Carved between 1441 and 1473, they represent the fully armoured infantrymen or marines who defended Italian colonial outposts around the Balkans. (in situ No. 18, Ulica Juja Barakovica, Sibenik; author's photographs)

gunners on how best to lay their guns. Previously they had fired at one point, but the ambassador taught then to fire three shots to form a triangle followed by a shot from one of the 'giant' guns which would bring down the weakened structure. Giacomo Tedaldi reported that the sultan's cannon fired between 100 and 150 times a day, consuming 1,100 lb (500 kg) of powder. The size of the cannonballs appalled those on the receiving end, and the ammunition was sufficiently valuable for Ottoman troops to risk using nets to drag them from the fosse to be used again.

Mehmet sent troops with lighter artillery to take the outlying Byzantine forts at Therapia and Studios. The Ottoman fleet's first attack upon the floating boom across the mouth of the Golden Horn was, however, a failure and Baltaoglu decided to await the arrival of additional ships from the Black Sea. On the 12th the Ottoman fleet was again driven off because the taller ships of the less numerous Christian fleet tried to encircle some Ottoman vessels.

On the night of 17–18 April the Ottomans launched a surprise night attack on the Mesoteichon sector of the land-walls, but after a four-hour battle the defenders drove them back. It was probably on the following day, perhaps to maintain Ottoman morale, that the fleet was sent to seize the Princes Islands. Two days later the Ottoman fleet suffered a serious reverse when three large Genoese-Papal transports carrying weapons, troops and food suddenly appeared off Constantinople accompanied by a large Byzantine ship carrying wheat from Sicily. They had sailed through the Dardanelles unreported and the furious sultan ordered Baltaoglu to capture them or not return alive. The Christians' sails apparently looked like islands rising from the sea of smaller Ottoman ships, which closed around them using oars alone because of a contrary

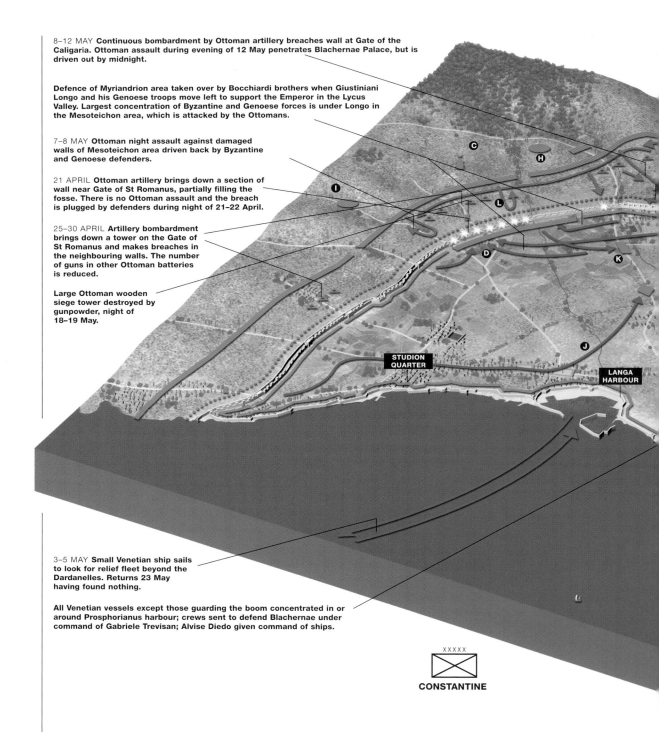

8–12 MAY Continuous bombardment by Ottoman artillery breaches wall at Gate of the Caligaria. Ottoman assault during evening of 12 May penetrates Blachernae Palace, but is driven out by midnight.

Defence of Myriandrion area taken over by Bocchiardi brothers when Giustiniani Longo and his Genoese troops move left to support the Emperor in the Lycus Valley. Largest concentration of Byzantine and Genoese forces is under Longo in the Mesoteichon area, which is attacked by the Ottomans.

7–8 MAY Ottoman night assault against damaged walls of Mesoteichon area driven back by Byzantine and Genoese defenders.

21 APRIL Ottoman artillery brings down a section of wall near Gate of St Romanus, partially filling the fosse. There is no Ottoman assault and the breach is plugged by defenders during night of 21–22 April.

25–30 APRIL Artillery bombardment brings down a tower on the Gate of St Romanus and makes breaches in the neighbouring walls. The number of guns in other Ottoman batteries is reduced.

Large Ottoman wooden siege tower destroyed by gunpowder, night of 18–19 May.

STUDION QUARTER

LANGA HARBOUR

3–5 MAY Small Venetian ship sails to look for relief fleet beyond the Dardanelles. Returns 23 May having found nothing.

All Venetian vessels except those guarding the boom concentrated in or around Prosphorianus harbour; crews sent to defend Blachernae under command of Gabriele Trevisan; Alvise Diedo given command of ships.

XXXXX
CONSTANTINE

THE SECOND PHASE OF THE SIEGE (21 APRIL TO 25 MAY 1453)

Many of the units defending the walls of Constantinople moved sideways or had a longer stretch of wall allocated to them. The Ottomans shocked the Byzantines by bringing their ships overland and launching them directly into the Golden Horn

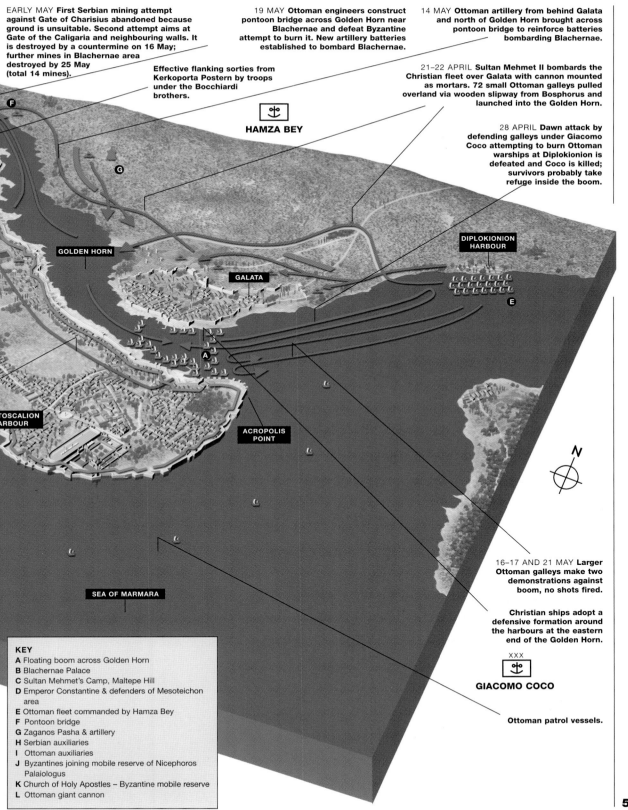

EARLY MAY **First Serbian mining attempt against Gate of Charisius abandoned because ground is unsuitable. Second attempt aims at Gate of the Caligaria and neighbouring walls. It is destroyed by a countermine on 16 May; further mines in Blachernae area destroyed by 25 May (total 14 mines).**

Effective flanking sorties from Kerkoporta Postern by troops under the Bocchiardi brothers.

19 MAY **Ottoman engineers construct pontoon bridge across Golden Horn near Blachernae and defeat Byzantine attempt to burn it. New artillery batteries established to bombard Blachernae.**

14 MAY **Ottoman artillery from behind Galata and north of Golden Horn brought across pontoon bridge to reinforce batteries bombarding Blachernae.**

21–22 APRIL **Sultan Mehmet II bombards the Christian fleet over Galata with cannon mounted as mortars. 72 small Ottoman galleys pulled overland via wooden slipway from Bosphorus and launched into the Golden Horn.**

28 APRIL **Dawn attack by defending galleys under Giacomo Coco attempting to burn Ottoman warships at Diplokionion is defeated and Coco is killed; survivors probably take refuge inside the boom.**

HAMZA BEY

F

G

GOLDEN HORN

GALATA

DIPLOKIONION HARBOUR

E

A

TOSCALION HARBOUR

ACROPOLIS POINT

SEA OF MARMARA

16–17 AND 21 MAY **Larger Ottoman galleys make two demonstrations against boom, no shots fired.**

Christian ships adopt a defensive formation around the harbours at the eastern end of the Golden Horn.

xxx

GIACOMO COCO

Ottoman patrol vessels.

KEY
A Floating boom across Golden Horn
B Blachernae Palace
C Sultan Mehmet's Camp, Maltepe Hill
D Emperor Constantine & defenders of Mesoteichon area
E Ottoman fleet commanded by Hamza Bey
F Pontoon bridge
G Zaganos Pasha & artillery
H Serbian auxiliaries
I Ottoman auxiliaries
J Byzantines joining mobile reserve of Nicephoros Palaiologos
K Church of Holy Apostles – Byzantine mobile reserve
L Ottoman giant cannon

wind. But their oars became entangled and the height of the Christian sailing ships gave their defenders a huge advantage. Baltaoglu's men could only try to board or burn the ships, and they failed on both counts. During the afternoon, however, the wind dropped and the battle drifted towards the shore, where the excited young sultan urged his horse into the sea as he shouted unhelpful, non-nautical orders to Baltaoglu. The latter pretended not to hear and drew back his smaller ships while the larger vessels with guns attacked the Christians. But their elevation was too low to hit the men on deck and their bore too small to seriously damage the hulls, so Baltaoglu reverted to boarding. The Ottoman admiral was wounded in the eye while Sultan Mehmet became ever angrier. Finally, as the sun set, the wind suddenly returned, the Christian ships pushed the smaller Ottoman craft aside and ran for the boom while three Venetian ships sailed out to cover the opening of the boom. Dusk was falling and, unable to reassemble his ships, Baltaoglu ordered them back to Diplokionion.

This highly visible defeat clearly had a serious impact on Ottoman morale while that of the defenders was raised. Turkish sources also refer to competing factions appearing within the Ottoman camp. So next day Baltaoglu was brought before the sultan and publicly threatened with execution. It is unlikely that Mehmet intended to kill such a brave and skilful commander and the testimony of fellow officers as to Baltaoglu's courage may have been prearranged. Nevertheless, heads had to roll and Baltaoglu was stripped of his rank, flogged, and replaced as commander

BELOW LEFT **This illustration from the late 15th-century Ottoman *Iskendername* shows one of Alexander's ships meeting another vessel at sea. Though stylised, the ships are basically realistic and are also in the Mediterranean rather than Indian ocean style. (Institute of Oriental Studies, Ms. C. 133, f.157b, St Petersburg)**

BELOW RIGHT **This little-known wall painting in the last large church to be built in Mistra, capital of the Byzantine Despotate of the Morea, shows an infantry archer with a recurved eastern-style composite bow and a quiver on his hip. On his head, however, the artist has given him a somewhat confused visored bascinet. (*in situ* Pantanassa Church, Mistra; author's photograph)**

of the fleet by Hamza Bey. Mehmet now summoned his commanders to Diplokionion to discuss the situation. Çandarli Halil advocated an offer to lift the siege in return for political rights over Constantinople and an annual tribute of 70,000 gold pieces. Zaganos Pasha, the other viziers and the sultan's spiritual adviser Shaykh Aq Shams al-Din, argued to continue the siege, with which the sultan agreed.

THE OTTOMANS TAKE THE GOLDEN HORN

The sultan had most of the cannon taken off the Ottoman ships and mounted ashore to bombard the Italians and Byzantines defending the boom. But most were shielded by the suburb of Galata. This was when Mehmet was credited with devising a new form of long-range mortar. An ordinary cannon was mounted at a very high angle and, according to Mehmet II's Greek biographer Kritovoulos, the sultan told them to 'get the measure by mathematical calculations' in an early example of the new science of ballistics.

Work was also started, or more probably speeded up, on the construction of a wooden slipway from the Bosphorus, across the hills behind Galata down to the Golden Horn. Since the Ottoman fleet had failed to force the boom, their smaller warships would be taken overland. Sultan Mehmet is generally assumed to have been copying what the

The ruins of the Byzantine Blachernae Palace are now known as the Tekfur Sarayi. The basic structure might date from the 12th century, but was modified over the years. (Author's photograph)

THE OTTOMANS LAUNCH GALLEYS INTO THE GOLDEN HORN (22 APRIL).

People in Constantinople were horrified to see a long line of Ottoman warships sliding down a long wooden slipway from the hill behind Galata. They had been hauled from the Bosphorus by teams of men and bullocks to a spot known as the Valley of the Springs, apparently ready for immediate action. As a result, the defenders lost control of the Golden Horn and the Ottoman galleys were able to threaten the northern walls of Constantinople.

ABOVE **The European shore of the Bosphorus near Tarabya. All vestiges of the late Byzantine outpost of Therapia seem to have disappeared. During the Byzantine era the area was largely neglected, only becoming fashionable after the Ottoman conquest. (Author's photograph)**

RIGHT **All that remains of Galata's medieval fortifications is the Galata Tower, which originally formed a strongpoint at the uppermost part of the town. In later centuries it served as a watch tower for the Ottoman fire brigade. Today the Galata Tower still looks down over a thriving commercial centre which appropriately includes the glass-covered Turkish offices of the Italian Banca di Roma. (Author's photograph)**

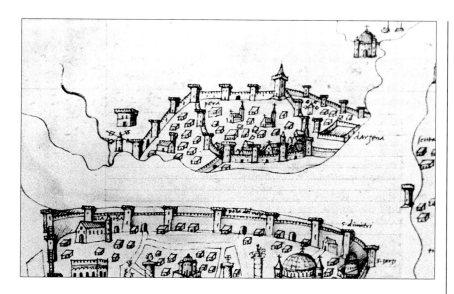

A slightly later copy of Cristofori Buondelmonti's book, *Liber Insularium*, includes a simplified version of his famous map of Constantinople. This section shows the Golden Horn with Genoese Galata above. To the left of Galata's wall a windmill stands in the Valley of the Springs, where the Ottomans launched their galleys. In the top right-hand corner is a church and two columns, marking the Diplokionion harbour, which the Ottoman navy made its headquarters during the siege.

Venetians had done some years earlier when they portaged a few galleys from the River Adige to the northern end of Lake Garda, but Muslim commanders had done something similar long before. Saladin transported warships in sections from the Nile to the Red Sea in the 12th century, and the Mamluks had taken disassembled galleys from Cairo to Suez as recently as 1424.

The lowest point behind Galata was almost 230 feet (70 metres) above sea level and the route taken by the Ottoman slipway was from present-day Tophane, up a steep valley to what is now Taksim Square, then down a valley to the Valley of the Springs, now called Kasimpasa. The slipway consisted of a planked wooden roadway in a shallow trench, greased like a ship-launching ramp. By 22 April it was complete and under cover of an artillery bombardment the ships were hauled across the hills on rollers then launched into the Golden Horn with their sails ready and skeleton crews aboard. Eventually, 72 of the Ottoman fleet's smaller craft, including 30 galleys, were lowered carefully down to the

Diplokionion Bay is now fronted by the Dolmabahçe Palace and a waterfront from which ferries cross to the Asiatic shore. The Ottoman galleys would probably have been dragged from the Bosphorus, where larger ships can be seen in the distance. (Author's photograph)

Valley of the Springs, thus leaving only the largest Ottoman ships in the Bosphorus. The defenders had lost control of the Golden Horn, and men had to be withdrawn from other sectors to defend the threatened walls facing the inlet; the investment of Constantinople was complete.

Presumably believing that the Ottoman fleet in the Bosphorus was now seriously weakened, the defenders attacked it with fire-ships. Two hours before dawn on 28 April a raiding party set out under the command of Giacomo Coco. His fleet consisted of two large transports packed with sacks of cotton and wool, accompanied by the galleys of Gabriele Trevisan and Zaccaria Grioni and three smaller ships. Coco then supposedly spoiled the plan by sailing impatiently ahead. The Ottoman ships opened fire and sunk Coco's vessel with all hands. Trevisan's galley was also hit but limped back to the Golden Horn. A violent naval battle lasted an hour and a half, with the Ottomans emerging victorious despite the loss of one ship.

Alvise Longo had set out from Venice on 19 April but only with one galley, not the 16 ships first envisaged. Even so he was ordered to wait in

the Aegean until Loredan arrived. Meanwhile, Emperor Constantine sent a scout ship to look for this relief fleet; a small vessel with a crew of 12 volunteers dressed as Turks and flying an Ottoman flag slipping out of Constantinople on 3 April. They saw no sign of help outside the Dardanelles and their report on 23 May threw Constantine into despair. For his part, Sultan Mehmet was worried that a fleet would, indeed, arrive from the west, and according to Giacomo Tedaldi, the nine galleys and 20 others ships which eventually assembled at Negroponte would have been enough to save Constantinople even if it had arrived a day before the city fell – but it did not.

On 3 May the defenders placed guns on the Golden Horn walls, hoping to drive back the Ottoman ships. More dramatic was the impact of Sultan Mehmet's newly devised long-range mortar, which opened fire on 5 May. At first its aim was inaccurate, but according to Kritivoulos: 'they fired again and this stone went to an immense height and came down with a tremendous crash and velocity, striking the galley in the centre...' The victim was an apparently neutral Genoese merchant ship moored close to Galata. It sank immediately.

Continued skirmishing in the Golden Horn eventually forced all the Christian ships except those guarding the boom to withdraw into the small Prosphorianus harbour, while their crews were sent to defend the Blachernae area. The boom itself remained a problem for the Ottoman fleet, which made unsuccessful attacks on 16–17 and 21 May. At the same time Ottoman engineers constructed a pontoon bridge further up the Golden Horn substantial enough to carry wagons and artillery. A Byzantine attempt to destroy this bridge with Greek Fire failed, and this new link between Ottoman forces on each side of the Horn proved very useful.

The bombardment of the land-walls continued, and on 2 May the mighty *Basiliske* was returned to its original position. On the 6th additional guns concentrated in batteries facing the St Romanus Gate sector made another breach. This was enlarged on the 7th, but was still only 10 feet (3 metres) wide and an Ottoman assault the following night failed. This seems to have been the occasion when, according to Alexander Ypsilanti using Balkan and Turkish sources, Ottoman soldiers under Murad Pasha seemed likely to break through until a Greek nobleman named Rhangabe cut off Murad's leg before himself falling. A general rout of the Byzantine defenders seemed possible until Giustiniani and the

voyvode Theodore joined in, followed by Emperor Constantine, Loukas Notaras and the *Eparch* Nicholas.

Between 8 and 11 May a new breach was made near the Caligaria Gate, followed by an evening assault on the 12th which penetrated the Blachernae Palace before being driven back. The Ottoman artillery was moved again, many pieces going to the St Romanus Gate sector, which looked the most promising. Nothing is heard of the stone-throwing mangonels, which were probably ineffective, but the Ottoman army did start to undermine the land-walls. Most of the miners were Serbians sent by the Serbian *Despot* and placed under Zaganos Pasha. Their first mine was towards the Charisian Gate, but this was in the Lycus Valley and the ground proved unsuitable, so the miners tried again, this time aiming for the Blachernae wall near the Caligarian Gate. A Byzantine counter-termine, excavated under the direction of Johannes Grant broke into the Serbian shaft on 16 May and further Ottoman mining efforts were defeated on 21 May, some flooded, some smoked out. On 23 May several miners and an Ottoman officer were captured underground. Under torture the officer revealed the location of the remaining mines and by 25 May all had been destroyed. Zaganos Pasha also had some large wooden siege towers constructed. They were not mobile,

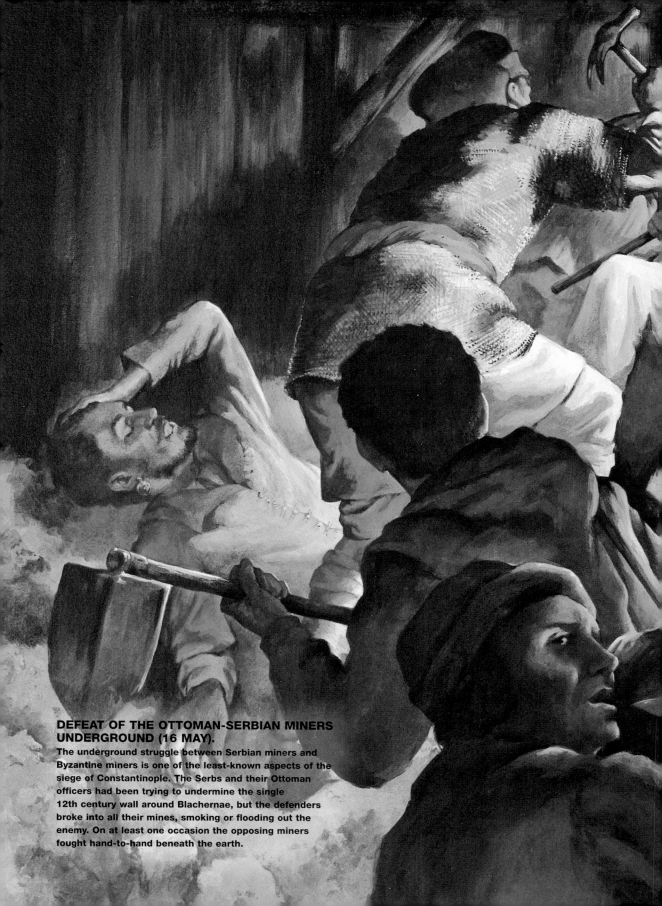

DEFEAT OF THE OTTOMAN-SERBIAN MINERS UNDERGROUND (16 MAY).
The underground struggle between Serbian miners and Byzantine miners is one of the least-known aspects of the siege of Constantinople. The Serbs and their Ottoman officers had been trying to undermine the single 12th century wall around Blachernae, but the defenders broke into all their mines, smoking or flooding out the enemy. On at least one occasion the opposing miners fought hand-to-hand beneath the earth.

but served as strongpoints and cover. One was blown up with barrels of gunpowder during a sudden sortie on the night of 18/19 May, and after others were destroyed by various means the rest were dismantled.

For their part, the defenders found it increasingly difficult to plug breaches in the Lycus Valley sector once the fosse had been largely filled. Instead, they erected stockades of rubble, earth and timber within the gaps. It was also increasingly difficult to launch sorties because the shattered gates made the defenders too visible. The Kerkoporta Postern was reopened, however, and used in successful flank attacks, mostly by cavalry under the Bocchiardi brothers, when Ottoman infantry attacked the northern sector.

Nevertheless, morale was declining inside Constantinople with increasing tension between Italian and Greek defenders. Worse still, the *Hodegetria*, the holiest icon in Constantinople, slipped from its platform while being carried in procession around the city. Next day, probably 12 May, an unseasonable fog shrouded the city and a strange effect of light hovered around the cathedral of Santa Sofia, causing concern in both camps. Muslim leaders declared that it

ABOVE **Kilyos, just west of the northern entrance of the Bosphorus. Turkish Thrace has few harbours and is exposed to the full force of gales sweeping down from Russia. Yet it was the last sizeable piece of adjacent territory remaining to Byzantine Constantinople in the mid-15th century. (Peter Lewis photograph)**

BELOW LEFT **Mamluk or Ottoman sword with down-turned dragons' heads quillons and a very heavy pommel. (Askeri Müze, inv. 2431, Istanbul; author's photograph)**

BELOW RIGHT **Ottoman or Mamluk sabre with a Middle Eastern hilt, 15th–16th century. (Askeri Müze, inv. 5306, Istanbul; author's photograph)**

was the Light of the True Faith which would soon shine within the ancient building. Some of the emperor's advisers suggested he leave and continue the struggle elsewhere. Mehmet II now sent a final embassy into Constantinople, led by his brother-in-law Isfendiyaroglu Ismail Bey, the vassal ruler of Kastamonu and Sinop who had friends amongst the Byzantine ruling élite. He presented the Ottoman terms: the emperor must retire to the Morea in southern Greece and the city must be handed over to Ottoman rule. But Constantine XI, according to later chroniclers, replied: 'God forbid that I should live as an Emperor without an Empire. As my city falls, I will fall with it. Whosoever wishes to escape, let him save himself if he can, and whoever is ready to face death, let him follow me.' In fact the Venetian fleet had left port and there were rumours that the Hungarians were preparing to march, which may have been why the emperor refused the sultan's terms.

THE FALL OF THE CITY

On 26 May Sultan Mehmet called a council of war. Çandarli Halil still argued in favour of a compromise and emphasised the continuing danger from the West, but Zaganos Pasha insisted that this time the Ottomans' western foes would not unite. He also pointed out that Mehmet's hero, Alexander the Great, had conquered half the world when still a young man. So Mehmet sent Zaganos Pasha to sound out the opinions of the men, perhaps knowing full well what answer he would bring. The following day Mehmet toured the army, while heralds announced a final assault by land

This extraordinary Byzantine carved wooden panel depicts a fleet of galleys and transport ships (right) attacking a town (left). Although this carving may not depict the Ottoman siege of Constantinople, it was made around the same time. (Rear of an icon of the Holy Spirit descending on the Apostles, Hermitage Museum, inv. J.428, St Petersburg)

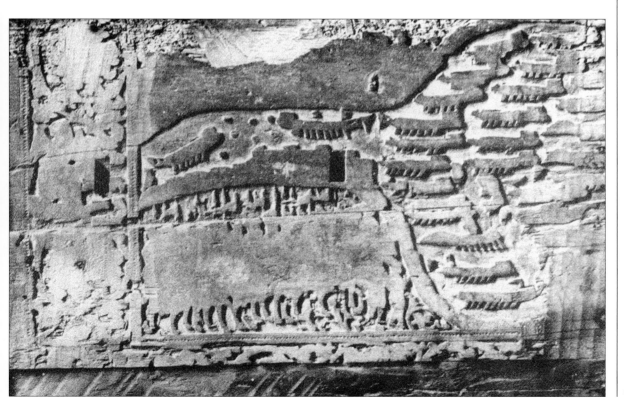

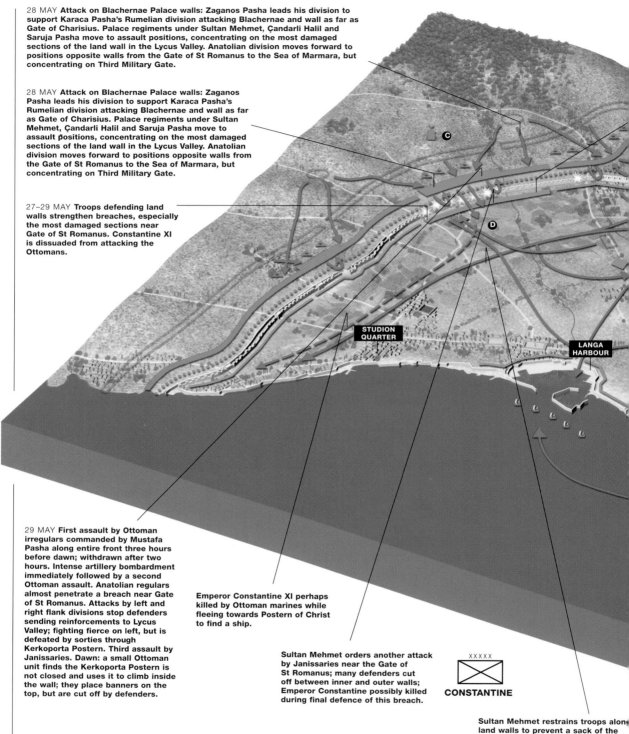

28 MAY Attack on Blachernae Palace walls: Zaganos Pasha leads his division to support Karaca Pasha's Rumelian division attacking Blachernae and wall as far as Gate of Charisius. Palace regiments under Sultan Mehmet, Çandarli Halil and Saruja Pasha move to assault positions, concentrating on the most damaged sections of the land wall in the Lycus Valley. Anatolian division moves forward to positions opposite walls from the Gate of St Romanus to the Sea of Marmara, but concentrating on Third Military Gate.

28 MAY Attack on Blachernae Palace walls: Zaganos Pasha leads his division to support Karaca Pasha's Rumelian division attacking Blachernae and wall as far as Gate of Charisius. Palace regiments under Sultan Mehmet, Çandarli Halil and Saruja Pasha move to assault positions, concentrating on the most damaged sections of the land wall in the Lycus Valley. Anatolian division moves forward to positions opposite walls from the Gate of St Romanus to the Sea of Marmara, but concentrating on Third Military Gate.

27–29 MAY Troops defending land walls strengthen breaches, especially the most damaged sections near Gate of St Romanus. Constantine XI is dissuaded from attacking the Ottomans.

C

D

STUDION QUARTER

LANGA HARBOUR

29 MAY First assault by Ottoman irregulars commanded by Mustafa Pasha along entire front three hours before dawn; withdrawn after two hours. Intense artillery bombardment immediately followed by a second Ottoman assault. Anatolian regulars almost penetrate a breach near Gate of St Romanus. Attacks by left and right flank divisions stop defenders sending reinforcements to Lycus Valley; fighting fierce on left, but is defeated by sorties through Kerkoporta Postern. Third assault by Janissaries. Dawn: a small Ottoman unit finds the Kerkoporta Postern is not closed and uses it to climb inside the wall; they place banners on the top, but are cut off by defenders.

Emperor Constantine XI perhaps killed by Ottoman marines while fleeing towards Postern of Christ to find a ship.

Sultan Mehmet orders another attack by Janissaries near the Gate of St Romanus; many defenders cut off between inner and outer walls; Emperor Constantine possibly killed during final defence of this breach.

XXXXX

CONSTANTINE

Sultan Mehmet restrains troops along land walls to prevent a sack of the city; sends units from the palace regiments to protect areas which surrender individually.

THE FINAL PHASE OF THE SIEGE (26 MAY TO 29 MAY 1453)

The final Ottoman assault was launched with great display on 29 May

Giustiniani Longo hands over command of Mesoteichon sector to Genoese officers and withdraws to his ship in the Golden Horn. Panic spreads among defenders of the land-walls.

Ottoman troops penetrate Blachernae and capture most of the defenders. Defenders of the Golden Horn walls see Ottoman troops behind them, and many escape across the wall; crews of Ottoman ships in Golden Horn enter Constantinople.

⚓
HAMZA BEY

Crews of many Ottoman ships break into Constantinople through the Platea and Horaia Gates and open other gates along the Golden Horn. Many Venetian crews escape to their ships.

28 MAY Ottoman fleet sails from Diplokionion to spread along the boom and Marmara walls as far as Langa harbour. Ottoman galleys in the Golden Horn are spaced along the shoreline of Constantinople. Zaganos Pasha sends some men to help galley crews in the Golden Horn.

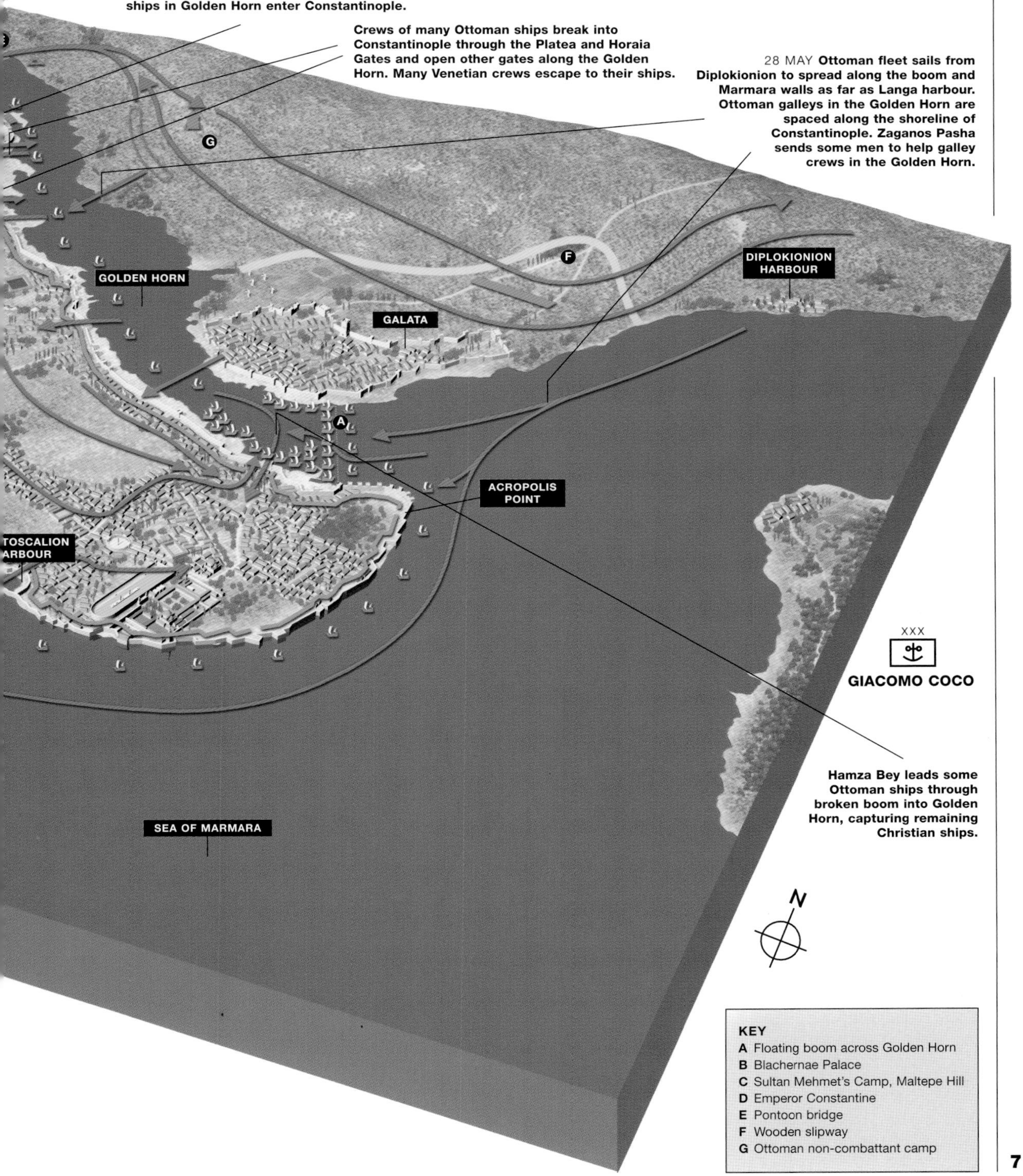

G

F

DIPLOKIONION HARBOUR

GOLDEN HORN

GALATA

A

ACROPOLIS POINT

TOSCALION ARBOUR

xxx
⚓
GIACOMO COCO

Hamza Bey leads some Ottoman ships through broken boom into Golden Horn, capturing remaining Christian ships.

SEA OF MARMARA

N

KEY
A Floating boom across Golden Horn
B Blachernae Palace
C Sultan Mehmet's Camp, Maltepe Hill
D Emperor Constantine
E Pontoon bridge
F Wooden slipway
G Ottoman non-combattant camp

71

and sea on 29 May. Celebration bonfires were lit and from 26 May there was continuous feasting in the Ottoman camp. Criers announced that the first man on to the wall of Constantinople would be rewarded with high rank, and religious leaders told the soldiers about the famous Companion of the Prophet Muhammad, Abu Ayyub (Eyüp in Turkish), who had died during the first Arab-Islamic attack upon Constantinople in 672. In fact, the defenders saw so many torches that some thought the enemy were burning their tents before retreating. At midnight all lights were extinguished and work ceased. The defenders, however, spent the night repairing and strengthening breaches in the wall. Giustiniani Longo also sent a message to Loukas Notaras, requesting his reserve of artillery. Notaras refused, Longo accused him of treachery and they almost came to blows until the emperor intervened.

The following day was dedicated to rest in the siege lines while Sultan Mehmet visited every unit including the fleet. Final orders were sent to the Ottoman commanders. Admiral Hamza Bey was to spread his ships around the sea-walls and erect scaling ladders where possible. Zaganos Pasha was to send men to help the ships in the Golden Horn while the

ABOVE (FROM LEFT TO RIGHT)
Bascinet with a rigid neckguard, a hinged part of which is missing, found in Halkis, 15th century. (Historical Museum, Athens; author's photograph)

Bascinet helmet with a rigid neckguard and an unusually small visor, found in Halkis, 15th century. (Historical Museum, Athens; author's photograph)

Italian salet of a form which almost entirely covers the wearer's face, Italian 15th century. (Askeri Müze, Istanbul; author's photograph)

Italian salet with a hinged nasal, Italian 15th century. (Historical Museum, Athens; author's photograph)

LEFT **In this illustration from a late 15th-century Ottoman copy of the *Iskendername*, Alexander arrives at the Ramini island. In the foreground is a simplified but clearly Mediterranean ship with a covered poop, probably modelled upon Ottoman vessels. (Institute of Oriental Studies, Ms. C. 133, f.100b, St Petersburg)**

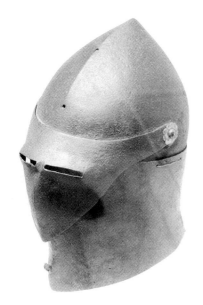  

rest crossed the pontoon bridge to assist the attack upon Blachernae. Karaca Pasha and the Rumelians would be on their right as far as the Gate of Charisius. Ishak Pasha and Mahmud Pasha with the Anatolians would attack between the Gate of St Romanus and the Marmara shore, massing around the Third Military Gate. Sultan Mehmet, Çandarli Halil and Saruja Pasha would direct the main attack in the Lycus Valley.

Late that afternoon as the setting sun shone in the defenders' eyes, the Ottomans began to fill the fosse while the artillery was brought as close as possible. The Ottoman ships in the Golden Horn spaced

RIGHT **Part of the Marmara walls of Constantinople near the Dëgirmen Kapi or Gate of St Barbara. They were not as strong as the land-walls and consisted of little more that a single wall with closely spaced towers. (Author's photograph)**

themselves between the Xyloporta and Horaia Gate, while those outside the boom spread more widely as far as the Langa harbour. It began to rain but work continued until around 1.30 in the morning of 29 May.

The defenders had also been rearranged to some extent. Manuel of Genoa, with 200 archers and crossbowmen, guarded districts around the Golden Gate and Studion; the scholar Theophilus Palaeologos commanded forces south of the Pege Gate, while Giovanni Giustiniani Longo with 400 Italians and the bulk of the Byzantine troops was responsible for the most threatened sector around the Gate of St Romanus. The Myriandrion area went to the brothers Antonio, Paolo and Troilo Bocchiardi. Girolamo Minotto was placed in command of the Blachernae Palace area where Theodorus from Karyston, described in Greek sources as 'the best archer on earth', and Johannes Grant, 'an able military engineer', defended the Caligaria Gate. Archbishop Leonard of Chios and a certain Hieronymus guarded the Xyloporta. Cardinal Isidore's men probably defended the walls to the right of the Xyloporta. Loukas Notaras took charge of the Petrion district as far as the Gate of St Theodosia, while 500 archers and hand-gunners manned walls facing the Golden Horn. Gabriele Trevisan commanded 50 soldiers who guarded the central section of Golden Horn walls, while the crews of Cretan ships manned those around the Horaia Gate, probably under Trevisan's command. Antonio Diedo retained command of the ships. The Catalan consul, Père Julia, defended the Bucoleon district as far as the Contoscalion. Prince Orhan was still stationed near the Langa harbour, while Jacopo Contarini's men defended the sea-walls of the Langa harbour and Psamathia.

The narrow and twisting Golden Horn seen from the Mosque of Eyüp. The northern end of the land-walls, around the Blachernae Palace, would have come down to the water next to the second slit of land protruding from the right.
(Author's photograph)

Demetrios Cantakuzenos, with his son-in-law Nicephoros Palaiologos and others, took up position at the Church of the Holy Apostles with reinforcements, while the emperor made tours of inspection to boost morale. Monks and clergy conducted constant religious services, and led processions within Constantinople and around its walls, quarrels apparently being forgotten as Orthodox and Latin Christians joined in prayer in Santa Sofia.

About three hours before dawn on 29 May there was a ripple of fire from the Ottoman artillery, and Ottoman irregulars swept forward led, according to Alexander Ypsilanti, by Mustafa Pasha. The main attack focused around the battered Gate of St Romanus, where Giustiniani Longo had taken 3,000 troops to the outer wall. Despite terrible casualties, few Ottoman volunteers retreated until, after two hours of fighting, Sultan Mehmet ordered a withdrawal. Ottoman ships similarly attempted to get close enough to erect scaling ladders, but generally failed.

After another artillery bombardment it was the turn of the provincial troops. They included Anatolian troops in fine armour who attacked the St Romanus Gate area at the centre. They marched forward carrying torches in the pre-dawn gloom, but were hampered by the narrowness of the breaches in Constantinople's walls. More disciplined than the irregulars, they occasionally pulled back to allow their artillery to fire, and during one such bombardment a section of defensive stockade was brought down. Three hundred Anatolians immediately charged through the gap but were driven off. Elsewhere fighting was particularly intense at the Blachernae walls. Alexander Ypsilanti again adds colourful details, stating that the *Beylerbeyi* of Anatolia sent five of his tallest soldiers against the breaches where they were met by the *protostrator* Giustiniani Longo and his 'sons' or the 'three brother-sons of *boyars*', probably meaning the Bocchiardi brothers. This second assault continued until an hour before dawn when it was called off.

ABOVE **The pommel of a fine sabre which was said to have been used by Sultan Mehmet II. The figure appears to be using a** *kamal*, **a primitive early form of sextant used by Islamic sailors through the Middle Ages. (Topkapi Armoury, Istanbul)**

LEFT **The most interesting panel on the frontispiece of the late 15th-century Ottoman** *Sulayman-Name* **manuscript represents the Prophet-King's army. The two officers on the left carry maces, one flanged, the other a transitional Turkish animal-headed style. (Chester Beatty Library, Dublin)**

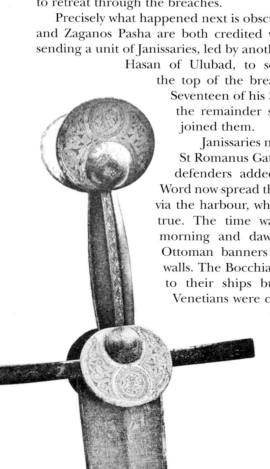

Sultan Mehmet now had only one fresh corps – his own palace regiments including the Janissaries. According to Ypsilanti, uncorroborated by any other known source, the 3,000 Janissaries were led by Baltaoglu as they attacked the main breach near the St Romanus Gate. All sources agree that these Janissaries advanced with terrifying discipline, moving slowly and without noise or music, while Sultan Mehmet accompanied them as far as the edge of the fosse. This third phase of fighting lasted an hour before some Janissaries on the left found that the Kerkoporta postern had not been properly closed after the last sortie. About 50 soldiers broke in, rushed up the internal stairs and raised their banner on the battlements. They were nevertheless cut off and were in danger of extermination when the Ottomans had a stroke of luck which their discipline and command structure enabled them to exploit fully.

Giovanni Giustiniani Longo was on one of the wooden ramparts in the breach when he was struck by a bullet. This went through the back of his arm into his cuirass, probably through the arm-hole – a mortal wound though none yet realised it – and he withdrew to the rear. The Emperor Constantine was nearby and called out: 'My brother, fight bravely. Do not forsake us in our distress. The salvation of the City depends on you. Return to your post. Where are you going?' Giustiniani simply replied: 'Where God himself will lead these Turks.' When Giustiniani's men saw him leave, they thought he was running away. Panic spread, spurred on by the sight of an Ottoman banner on the wall to the north; and those outside the main walls rushed back in an attempt to retreat through the breaches.

Precisely what happened next is obscured by legend. Sultan Mehmet and Zaganos Pasha are both credited with seeing the confusion and sending a unit of Janissaries, led by another man of giant stature named Hasan of Ulubad, to seize the wall. Hasan reached the top of the breach but was felled by a stone. Seventeen of his 30 comrades were also slain but the remainder stood firm until other soldiers joined them.

Janissaries now took the inner wall near the St Romanus Gate and by appearing behind the defenders added still further to their panic. Word now spread that the Ottomans had broken in via the harbour, which may or may not have been true. The time was about four o'clock in the morning and dawn was breaking as yet more Ottoman banners appeared on the Blachernae walls. The Bocchiardi brothers cut their way back to their ships but Minotto and most of the Venetians were captured. According to Doukas, the defenders of the Golden Horn wall escaped over the wall while Ottoman sailors swarmed in the opposite direction.

The defence now collapsed. Foreigners tried to reach their ships in the

LEFT **This illustration of a religious debate in the presence of Sultan Orhan, in the late 15th-century *Iskendername*, provided one of the earliest Ottoman representations of Ottoman costume or uniform. (Institute of Oriental Studies, Ms. C. 133, f.249b, St Petersburg)**

BELOW **The wall of the Blachernae Palace area was added outside the main line of Constantinople's Theodosian walls in the 12th century. Though only one wall deep and lacking a fosse or moat, it was of a more modern design which proved capable of resisting Sultan Mehmet's cannon. (Author's photograph)**

ABOVE **Few tourists venture into the run-down region around the Gül Camii, Mosque of the Rose, which incorporates an earlier Byzantine church. The steep slopes leading down to the Golden Horn were still densely populated in the mid-15th century. (Author's photograph)**

RIGHT **The role of a band of Ottoman soldiers who clambered up on to the main wall through the partially open Kerkoporta Postern was vital to the conquest of Constantinople. This postern stood at the junction of the Theodosian walls on the right and those of the Blachernae on the left, where a gap in the land-walls is now marked by a dark tree. (Author's photograph)**

Golden Horn while local Greek militiamen hurried to defend their own homes. Many defenders in the Lycus Valley were captured. The Studion and Psamathia quarters surrendered to the first proper Ottoman troops who appeared, and so retained their churches undamaged. The Catalans below the Old Palace were all killed or captured, which suggests they were cut off when Ottoman sailors broke through the Plataea and Horaia gates. Prince Orhan tried to escape disguised as a monk but was captured, pushed into the hold of a ship with other prisoners, and was later recognised and executed. Loukas Notaras was apparently a prisoner in the same ship, but was taken to Mehmet alive.

Giustiniani Longo was having his wounds dressed when news of the collapse arrived, so he recalled his men by trumpet. Cardinal Isidore

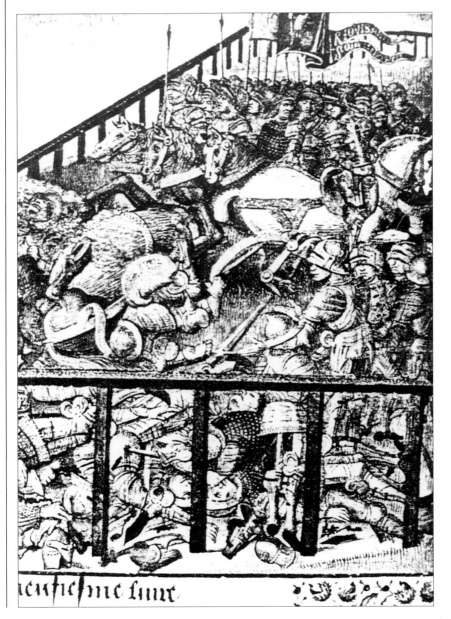

'A Fury terrifies the horse of Arcitas,' in a Franco-Burgundian manuscript. This copy of Boccaccio's *Theseide* was made around 1470 and seems to include a number of interesting items of arms and armour associated with Byzantine or Graeco-Italian light cavalry but not normally seen elsewhere. (Nat. Bib., Ms. 2617, Vienna)

The statue of Orlando, made by Bonino of Milan in 1413, was a symbol of the strength and independence of the merchant republic of Dubrovnik. It is also a fine illustration of the Italian-style armour worn by the military élite of the eastern Balkans and Constantinople.

disguised himself as a slave and escaped to Galata. Alvise Diedo crossed to Galata to discuss the situation and the Genoese authorities tried to arrest him, but so many Genoese sailors wanted to escape home that they forced their leaders to reopen the gates. Two sailors cut the floating boom and many Christian ships escaped under the command of Diedo. Others sailed out later in the day, including one carrying Giustiniani Longo, who died on his way home. Those ships which remained were captured by Hamza Bey, who with the crews still under his command led some galleys through the now broken boom into the Golden Horn. Cretan sailors manning three towers near the Horaia Gate held out until the early afternoon, refusing to surrender until the ships had escaped. Sultan Mehmet was so impressed by their dedication that he allowed them to return to their own ships and to sail away unhindered. Their captains were Sguros, Antonios Hyalinas and Philomates.

There are two basic versions of the death of the Emperor Constantine XI. One maintains that he and his companions charged into the fray as Ottoman soldiers poured through the main breach near the St Romanus Gate. Constantine supposedly shouted: 'Is there no Christian here who will take my head?' before being struck in the face and back. A different version is recounted by Tursun Bey and Ibn Kemal. This suggests that a band of naval *azaps* had dressed themselves as Janissaries so that they could enter the city after Mehmet issued his order preventing any but authorised units going beyond the main wall. They then came across the emperor near the Golden Gate and killed him before realising who he was. Perhaps Constantine was heading towards a tiny harbour just inside the point where the Sea of Marmara walls joined the land-walls, looking for a boat to take him to the *Despotate* of the Morea.

It is clear that some areas inside Constantinople resisted the first looters before surrendering to regular troops who were sent into the city while the bulk of the army remained outside. Mehmet's soldiers now advanced methodically, taking control and protecting each quarter from looters. Nevertheless, sailors or marines did enter via the other walls, looting Constantinople on a massive scale before regular troops forcibly stopped them. The rich Orthodox churches and monasteries suffered worst, but the survival of the Church of the Holy Apostles, despite being on the main road to the centre of the city, suggests that the sultan intended to keep it as the main Orthodox church while converting Santa Sofia into Constantinople's greatest mosque. In fact the ordinary people were treated better by their Ottoman conquerors than their ancestors had been by Crusaders back in 1204; only about 4,000 Greeks died in the siege. Many members of the élite fled into Santa Sofia, apparently believing an ancient prophecy that the infidels would

The Gate of Charius, now called the Edirne Kapi, has been accurately restored. This was where Sultan Mehmet II made his ceremonial entry into Constantinople, and it is still of great significance to the Turks. (Author's photograph)

turn tail at the last minute and be pursued back beyond Persia. Instead, Ottoman looters broke down the doors and dragged the people off for ransom.

The sultan himself remained outside the land-walls until about noon on 29 May, when he finally rode to Santa Sofia. There he stopped further damage, had the venerable building converted into a mosque, then joined other worshippers in afternoon prayers. According to Tursun Bey, Mehmet went outside the dome to survey the decrepit state of Constantinople and quote a verse by the Persian poet Firdawsi: 'The spider serves as gate-keeper in Khusrau's hall, the owl plays his music in the palace of Afrasiyab.' Later that afternoon Loukas Notaras was brought before the sultan and apparently reported that the Grand Vizier, Çandarli Halil, had been encouraging the defenders to resist during the course of the siege. In return Mehmet promised to place the old man at the head of the city's civil administration. Mehmet also had a list of captured officials drawn up and personally paid their ransoms.

On 30 May Sultan Mehmet took the opportunity of removing his independent-minded Grand Vizier, Çandarli Halil. He was replaced by the ultra-loyal Zaganos Pasha, who next day negotiated the surrender of Galata. On 1 June the outlying castles of Silivri and Epibatos surrendered peacefully. Mehmet also ordered all looting to stop and sent his troops back outside the walls. The siege was concluded.

AFTERMATH AND RECKONING

ESCAPE, RANSOM OR EXECUTION

On 5 June, long before he heard the awful news, the Pope finally agreed to pay the Venetian Senate 14,000 ducats to hire and crew five galleys for four months. The Venetian galleys, already on their way to Constantinople, were waiting at Chios for a suitable wind. There they heard of the fall of Constantinople from some Genoese ships which had escaped. The Venetian fleet under Loredan similarly stopped at Negroponte when it heard the news. In Constantinople itself, Girolomo Minotto and his sons were executed for fighting on after the city had surrendered. Loukas Notaras was also executed five days after the fall, largely because the Ottoman ruling élite distrusted all Byzantine officials and wanted them removed.

Mehmet probably left Constantinople on 18 June, arriving back in Edirne on the 21st. Çandarli Halil was now imprisoned, perhaps as the result of rumours about his loyalty, and was executed 40 days after the

The so-called Tabak Kapi or Gate of the Tanneries, also known as the Postern of Christ, marked the point where the massive land-walls of Constantinople joined the rather weaker sea-walls along the Marmara coast. (Author's photograph)

submission of the Gattilusi-ruled coastal enclave of Ainos (now Enez), in other words, late August or early September. Senior Byzantine and Italian captives were similarly taken back to Edirne, though Loukas Notaras' younger son soon escaped to join his sisters in Italy. Zaganos Pasha had meanwhile cultivated good relations with the Italians by paying the ransoms of 47 senior captives at 1,000 to 2,000 ducats each. Jacopo Contarini cost him 7,000 but all 29 Venetian noblemen were ransomed within the year. According to a Senate report, 40 noblemen and over 500 other Venetian citizens died during the siege. Venice looked after its own and, as was normal, the Senate voted pensions for the families of those killed and damages for those who had lost property. It cost the massive sum of 200,000 ducats. At the same time the Senate was informed that the Emperor Constantine owed Venice 17,163 *hyperpyra* when he died.

A MULTI-CULTURAL EMPIRE

The impact of the conquest upon the Ottoman Empire was profound and affected almost every area of life, from culture to politics, economics to military affairs. The *ghaza*, or war, with neighbouring Christian states soon focused more upon the Ottoman sultan's actions rather than upon the autonomous, often unorthodox frontier heroes of earlier days. Sultan Mehmet II concentrated his attention upon the reconstruction of his new capital. The walls were repaired and Constantinople was repopulated with Christian Greeks, Muslim Turks and others. Some were encouraged by tax privileges, but many were forced to settle in the largely empty city. This rapid population growth led to food shortages, which in turn led first to the conquest of grain-producing regions north of the Black Sea.

Naturally, the conquest of the city was followed by a substantial building programme, which produced a new palace, a remarkable hospital with students and medical staff, a large cultural complex, two sets of barracks for the Janissaries, and a *Tophane* gun foundry outside Galata. Sultan Mehmet wanted to make Constantinople a multi-faith centre for all 'peoples of the Book', Muslims, Christians and Jews alike. This grand imperial statement created a cross-roads where the cultures of East and West, Europe and Asia, met and mingled. A new Ottoman Constantinople, or Istanbul as it was called by the Turks, flourished until the tragic nationalism of the 19th century culminated in a massive separation of populations in the early 20th century. Galata, on the other side of the Golden Horn, remained western

BELOW **A militia formed from the ordinary citizens of Constantinople and perhaps peasants who had fled from the surrounding countryside fought alongside professional soldiers in the final defence of the city. Such armed peasants and shepherds are shown in late 15th-century wall paintings in northern Greece. (***in situ* **Old Katholikon of the Great Meteoreon, Meteora)**

European in population and culture. Only a few years after the conquest, the Turkish historian, Tursun Bey, could write: 'How curious is this city of Istanbul. For one copper coin one can be rowed from Rum-eli into Frankistan,' meaning that a cheap ferry ride could take a person from cosmopolitan Istanbul to still largely Italian Galata.

Furthermore, Sultan Mehmet II declared himself to be the new *Qaysar* or Caesar, the legitimate heir to the Roman and Byzantine empires with a claim to territory far beyond the Ottoman Empire's existing frontier. This was widely accepted, not only by the sultan's Turkish and Muslim subjects, but also by Greek scholars such as George of Trebizond, who wrote to Mehmet in 1466: 'No one doubts that you are the Emperor of the Romans. Whoever is legally master of the capital of the Empire is the Emperor and Constantinople is the capital of the Roman Empire.'

A SHOCK FOR CHRISTENDOM

The conquest of Constantinople cut Italian trade through the Dardanelles and Bosphorus to the Crimea. As early as 28 November 1453, the Genoese consul in Kaffa reported that extreme measures would be needed if his outpost was not to be entirely deserted, and there was soon a substantial emigration from all the Genoese Black Sea colonies. Many Armenians moved to the Ukraine or Poland, some Italian craftsmen went as far as Moscow, and within 20 or so years, all Genoa's possessions beyond the Bosphorus had been lost to the Ottomans.

The impact of the fall of Constantinople on the Byzantine world was, of course, catastrophic and many Orthodox Christians blamed it on the disloyalty of the Byzantine military élite. Conversion to Islam was never as widespread in Greek-speaking communities as among Slavs and Albanians, but it became quite common in what had been the Byzantine aristocracy. Conversion was even commonplace among the clergy, whose faith may have been shaken by what many saw as 'divine punishment'. In the immediate aftermath of the fall of Constantinople, however, much of the Byzantine élite fled; some to the tiny principality of Theodore Mangoup in the Crimea, some to Byzantine Trebizond, others to the Morea. Morea, however, was torn apart by internal dissension and rebellion between and against the co-*Despots*, and between Greeks and Albanians.

In October 1454 Mehmet II sent Turahan Bey to help the *Despots* Thomas and Demetrios, but as soon as they left, civil war flared up. In 1460 the Despotate of the Morea was finally incorporated directly into the Ottoman Empire, the capital, Mistra, falling exactly seven years after Constantinople, on 29 May 1460.

BELOW **Two Janissaries with their distinctive white felt caps hanging down the back of their necks are shown in this Ottoman** *Kulliyat* **manuscript made around 1480. The other four figures wear ordinary Ottoman court dress. (Topkapi Lib., Ms. Revan 989, f.230v, Istanbul)**

THE DEATH OF EMPEROR CONSTANTINE XI

The final moments of the last Emperor of Byzantium are shrouded in legend. The most 'heroic' version has him charging bare-headed into the breach, seeking death once he knew that Constantinople was lost and calling out: 'Is there no Christian here who will take my head?' Another version maintains that he was cut down while trying to escape, perhaps to a tiny harbour in the south-western corner of the city. He is shown here to the left of the picture, raising his sword in defiance as a Turk prepares to strike him from behind.

With the exception of Venetian enclaves that the Ottomans were not yet strong enough to take, the Latin possessions in Greece also fell, Athens being given special privileges because of Mehmet II's interest in ancient Greek civilisation. Some of the Genoese outposts in the Aegean lasted longer, Ainos remaining under Gattilusi rule. Palamedes Gattilusi was also entrusted with the island of Imroz, while the island of Lemnos was allocated to Dorino I Gattilusi, the lord of Mytilini, who ruled under Ottoman suzerainty and paid an annual tribute. In 1460 Ainos was given to the deposed co-*Despot* of the Morea, Demetrios. Elsewhere, the Gattilusio family retained Lesbos, under Ottoman suzerainty, until 1462, while a Genoese *Maona* or 'merchant commune' held the island of Chios until 1566, when the sultan handed it over to the Jewish Duke Joseph Nasi of Naxos.

Following the fall of Constantinople a series of campaigns confirmed Ottoman domination of the Balkans, although a clash with Hungary led to an Ottoman reverse outside Belgrade in 1456. Elsewhere, George Castriota (Iskander Beg or Skanderbeg) continued to resist the Ottomans in Albania until 1468. Wallachia moved more firmly beneath Ottoman suzerainty and even Moldavia was theoretically a tributary of the sultan after 1456. The following year Stefan the Great came to the throne of Moldavia, and spent much of his reign competing with the Ottomans for domination over Wallachia.

Further west the Ottoman conquest of Constantinople caused deep shock. Renaissance humanists were appalled that Greece now lay under Turkish domination, as the scholar Aeneas Sylvius Piccolomini (the future Pope Pius II) wrote: 'Here is a second death for Homer and for Plato too ... Now Muhammad reigns amongst us. Now the Turk hangs over our very heads.' Even though some writers pointed out that the Ottomans were good and honest people, horrendous propaganda soon led to the popular image of 'the Terrible Turk'. Ottoman victories were seen as unnatural, along with the Turks' supposedly blind obedience to their officers. Nevertheless, most Europeans still felt secure behind the powerful Catholic kingdom of Hungary, and the fate of the Orthodox Christians was regarded as God's punishment for their weakness and sin. Only when Hungary collapsed in the early 16th century did the rest of Europe fully awake to the danger from the East.

A final page from the late 15th-century Ottoman *Iskendername* epic poem illustrates the execution of Makhar and Makhyar. This was the fate of many senior men, Byzantine and Ottoman, after the fall of Constantinople. (Institute of Oriental Studies, Ms. C. 133, f.35b, St Petersburg)

THE BATTLEFIELD TODAY

Most of the action during the siege of Constantinople took place in one of today's leading tourist destinations, Istanbul. This superb city has abundant hotels in all categories, though camping facilities are distant from the centre. Food is cheap and transport in the form of Istanbul's efficient water buses is something not to be missed. Boats also link Istanbul with the Asiatic shore, practically every village along the Bosphorus and various places on the Sea of Marmara. Many of the buildings which existed in 1453 still survive, including most of the land-walls, the Marmara walls and some fragments of the Golden Horn walls. But the area within these defences is now almost filled with bustling residential and business quarters. Only in a few areas, inside the southern part of the land-walls is there still open land. Suburbs extend far beyond the medieval walls, while Galata has been swallowed by an urban sprawl which stretches far up the Bosphorus. Fortunately, a large part of the area where the Ottoman army established its siege lines remains open, except for the pleasant suburb of Eyüp outside the Blachernae walls.

In contrast to the tourist magnet of Istanbul, eastern Thrace is strangely neglected. The previous Ottoman capital of Edirne, where Sultan Mehmet II prepared his campaign, lies close to the Bulgarian and Greek frontiers. It has adequate hotels and retains the quiet charm which overcrowded Istanbul has largely lost. The Marmara coast, which was still in Byzantine hands at the start of the campaign, includes several seaside resorts, whereas the Black Sea coast of Thrace is virtually undeveloped, lacking even a coastal road. This area was, of course, a vulnerable frontier zone in Cold War days, but north of the border the Bulgarians have exploited the tourist potential of their coast, including towns that were Byzantine in 1453.

CHRONOLOGY

1437 Byzantine Emperor John VIII seeks support in Italy.

1439 Çandarli Halil Pasha made Grand Vizier, Ishak Pasha Second Vizier, Zaganos Pasha Third Vizier; Metropolitan Isidore of Kiev signs decree of Union between Orthodox and Latin churches at the Council of Ferrara-Florence.

1442 Janos Hunyadi, the Hungarian *voyvode* of Transylvania, defeats Ottomans in Wallachia.

1443 Spring: 11-year-old Prince Mehmet made governor of Amasya; Janos Hunyadi leads Crusading army into Balkans; Sultan Murad II campaigns against Karaman but makes peace and returns to face Hunyadi.

1444 Karaman invades Ottoman provinces in Anatolia; revolt against Ottoman rule spreads in Albania; death of Murad II's favourite son Alauddin Bey.
12 June: Peace between Murad II and Janos Hunyadi.
August: Murad II abdicates in favour of Mehmet II and retires to Bursa to ensure Mehmet's succession against the pretender Prince Orhan in Constantinople.
September: Byzantine *Despots* of the Morea invades central Greece; Crusader army breaks peace agreement and invades Ottoman territory; Islamic rising against Mehmet II in Edirne.
October: Murad II reassumes military leadership.
10 November: Ottomans defeat Hunyadi and Crusaders at battle of Varna.

1446 Murad II returns to throne; Mehmet II retains title of sultan but only acts as governor of Manisa; Ottoman campaigns re-establish Ottoman authority in Balkans and force Byzantine *Despots* of Morea to accept Ottoman suzerainty.

1448 **17–20 October:** Ottomans defeat Hungarian Crusaders at second battle of Kosovo and reimpose suzerainty on Wallachia.

1449 Death of Emperor John VIII; Constantine XI Palaiologos becomes Byzantine emperor; Heraclea on Marmora taken by Ottomans.

1451 Death of Murad II; Mehmet II becomes sultan for second time; Heraclea on Marmora probably returned to Byzantines; Ibrahim Bey of Karaman invades disputed area and instigates various revolts against Ottoman rule; Mehmet II conducts first campaign against Ibrahim of Karaman; Byzantines threaten to release Ottoman claimant Orhan.

1452 **14 February:** Venice agrees to send gunpowder and armour to Constantinople.
15 April–31 Aug: Ottomans build Rumeli Hisar which encourages the Venetian Senate to arm transport ships to be ready to sail on 8 April 1453 accompanied by 15 galleys. Venice also alerts warships in the Aegean and sends an embassy to discover the sultan's intentions
28 August: Mehmet II examines the walls of Constantinople then returns to Edirne.
Autumn: Mehmet II start assembling troops at Edirne; Byzantine emperor gathers grain and people into Constantinople.
1 September: Mehmet II arrives at Edirne; Hungarian gunfounder Urban transfers from Byzantine to Ottoman service and starts making giant cannon in Edirne.
6 September: Ottoman fleet returns to Gallipoli from Bosphorus.
October: Mehmet II sends troops to raid Byzantine Morea; Cardinal Isidore arrives in Constantinople with 200 archers.
November: Concern about Rumeli Hisar leads Genoa to send Giovanni Giustiniani Longo with men and ships to Constantinople.
10 November: Two Venetian merchant ships from the Black Sea pass Rumeli Hisar under fire.
25 November: Venetian ship from the Black Sea is sunk by gunfire from Rumeli Hisar.
December: Venetian galley from Trebizond under command of Giacomo Coco sails through the Bosphorus under fire; Venetian council in Constantinople agrees that no Venetian ships should leave without permission.
12 December: Joint Orthodox-Latin religious service in Santa Sofia cathedral and agreement to a Union of the Churches.

1452–53 Winter: Byzantine emperor sends ships to purchase food and military equipment in the Aegean; Byzantine galleys pillage Turkish coastal villages in the Sea of Marmara; defences of Constantinople repaired; Karaca Bey of Rumelia strengthens roads from Edirne to

OPPOSITE **The cathedral of Santa Sofia, now the Aya Sofia Mosque, was in many ways the symbol of Byzantine Constantinople. Not surprisingly Sultan Mehmet II Fatih, 'the Conqueror', came here immediately after ceremonially entering the city. (Author's photograph)**

91

Constantinople, and cuts down vineyards and orchards around the walls of the city; Ottoman units from Anatolia keep watch on Constantinople; Mehmet plans siege of Constantinople.

1453 January: Mehmet returns to Edirne from Didimotikon; Genoese galleys with 700 soldiers under Giovanni Giustiniani Longo arrive in Constantinople; Giustiniani made commander of land defences.

February: Ottoman advance guard under Karaca Bey storms Byzantine forts of Studius and Therapia.

26 February: Six ships escape from Golden Horn carrying 700 people.

Spring: Ottoman heavy guns brought from Edirne to face walls of Constantinople; Karaca Bey captures several towns on Black Sea and Marmora coast leaving only Selymbria and Epibatos, which resist and are bypassed.

March: Ottoman fleet assembles off Gallipoli and sails into Marmara; Anatolian troops cross Bosphorus via Rumeli Hisar.

23 March: Mehmet II leaves Edirne with palace regiments.

Late March-early April: Pope sends three Genoese ships to Constantinople with arms and provisions but these are storm-bound at Chios.

2 April: Chain drawn across Golden Horn; Mehmet II arrives in front of Constantinople.

6 April: Ottomans moves forward from assembly positions to within a mile of the walls of Constantinople; Byzantine defenders take up positions around walls.

9 April: First Ottoman naval attack on boom unsuccessful.

9 April or thereabouts: Ottoman troops take Therapia and Studios.

11 April: Erection of large mangonels in front of walls; giant Ottoman gun called *Basiliske* fires first shot.

12 April: Second Ottoman naval attack on boom unsuccessful.

15 April: Large Byzantine vessel and the three Genoese-Papal warships delayed by contrary winds, sail from Chios.

16 April or thereabouts: Ottoman fleet reinforced by large ships from northern Anatolia.

17–18 April (night): Ottoman surprise attack driven back.

18 April: Ottoman attack on Mesoteichon area; Ottoman fleet occupies Princes Islands.

19 April: Alvise Longo sails from Venice with one galley instead of proposed fleet of 16; possibly five others sail after 7 May.

20 April: Large Byzantine vessel and three Genoese-Papal warships break through Ottoman blockade into Constantinople.

21 April: Baltaoglu replaced as commander of the Ottoman fleet; cannon removed from Ottoman ships and placed on northern side of Golden Horn; council of war near Diplokionion decides to continue the siege; large tower near St Romanos Gate collapses but sultan not present to order an immediate assault; Mehmet devises a high-angle mortar.

22 April: Ottomans complete slipway from Bosphorus and launch smaller warships into the Golden Horn.

25–27 April: Ottoman guns make further breaches in the walls.

28 April: Christian ships try to burn Ottoman fleet in Diplokionion harbour but are defeated.

29 April: Byzantines behead 260 Ottoman prisoners.

30 April: Ottoman guns make a breach at the St Romanus Gate.

May: Emperor collects more funds from churches to buy food for troops; Serbian miners from Novo Brodo start excavating mines towards Charisian Gate, abandoned as ground unsuitable.

2 May: Great gun *Basiliske* returned to its original position.

3 May: Byzantines place guns on wall to attack Ottoman ships in Golden Horn; Emperor Constantine sends small ship beyond the Dardanelles to seek news of the Venetian relief fleet.

5 May: Ottoman high-angle mortar fires over Galata and sinks 'neutral' Genoese ship in Golden Horn.

6 May: Ottoman giant gun repaired; additional guns added to the St Romanus battery make another breach.

7–8 May (night): Ottoman night assault on breach at St Romanus Gate fails.

9–13 May: Venetian ships in Golden Horn unload war material and are mostly concentrated in the small Prosphorianus harbour.

10 May: Alvise Diedo given command of ships in harbour while Gabriele Trevisan takes spare crews to help defend Blachernae.

11 May: Loredan's ship leaves Venice.

12–13 May (night): Ottoman assault penetrates Blachernae Palace, but is driven out.

14 May: Ottomans win full control of Golden Horn then move guns from Valley of the Springs to reinforce those bombarding Blachernae.

16 May: Guns from Valley of the Springs not effective against Blachernae so they are sent to join the main batteries in the Lycus Valley; Ottoman mines beneath Blachernae wall are discovered and defeated.

16–17 May: Ottoman fleet makes demonstration against boom, no shots fired.

18–19 May (night): Ottoman wooden towers to protect men filling the fosse are destroyed by kegs of gunpowder; other are then dismantled.

19 May: Ottomans complete construction of pontoon bridge across upper part of Golden Horn.

21 May: Ottoman ships attack boom but withdraw when fail to take defenders by surprise.

23 May: Byzantines capture a senior Ottoman officer in a mine beneath Blachernae; under torture he reveals other mines; small boat returns from reconnaissance beyond the Dardanelles bringing news that no relief fleet is in sight.

24 May: Lunar eclipse worries both sides; Constantine refuses final surrender terms, Mehmet announces final assault within five days.

May, last week: Morale is breaking in Constantinople; holiest icon of Mother of God slips from platform during procession; peculiar fog and light appear over Santa Sofia.

25 May: Byzantine destroy last of Ottoman mines.

26 May: Ottomans hear rumours of approaching European relief army; Mehmet II holds council with senior men and sends Zaganos to assess morale of troops.

27 May: Mehmet II tours the army and heralds announce final attack.

27–28 May (night): Celebration fires lit in Ottoman camp because of forthcoming attack, weapons stockpiled.

28 May: Day of prayer and rest in Ottoman camp; Mehmet tours fronts; church services and religious processions within Constantinople; late afternoon Ottoman troops start final filling in the fosse and bring cannon to close range.

28–29 May (night): Ottoman ships brought as close as possible to the sea walls.

29 May: Final Ottoman assault starts about 1.30 am, breaking through around 4 am; Mehmet II prevents a general sack of the city, but sailors and auxiliaries enter from other directions; some quarters surrender on terms; Mehmet enters Constantinople early afternoon.

30 May: Çandarli Halil replaced as Grand Vizier by Zaganos Pasha.

1 June: Mehmet II has looting stopped and Ottoman army is ordered back to camp; Byzantine garrisons at Silivri and Epibatos surrender peacefully; Galata surrenders to Ottoman rule, though retains commercial rights.

3 June: Start of demolition of Galata's land-walls; execution of Loukas Notaras.

9 June: Cretan ships reach home with first news of the fall of Constantinople.

FURTHER READING

Babingen, F., *Mehmet the Conqueror and his Time* (Princeton 1978).

Bakapoulos, A., 'Les Limites de l'Empire Byzantin depuis la fin du XIVe siècles jusqu'à sa chute (1453),' *Byzantinische Zeitschrift* LV (1962) 56–65.

Barbaro, Nicolo (trans. J.R. Melville Jones), *Diary of the Siege of Constantinople* (New York 1969).

Browning, R., 'A Note on the Capture of Constantinople in 1453,' *Byzantion* XXII (1952) 379–387.

Concasty, M-L., 'Les Informations de Jacques Tedaldi sur le siège et la prise de Constaninople,' *Byzantion* XXIV (1954), 95–110.

De Vries, K., 'Gunpowder Weapons at the Siege of Constantinople, 1453,' in Y. Lev (edit.), *War and Society in the Eastern Mediterranean, 7th-15th Centuries* (Leiden 1996) 343–362.

Doukas (trans. H.J. Magoulias), *Decline and Fall of Byzantium to the Ottoman Turks* (Detroit 1975).

Dujcev, I., 'La conquête turque et la prise de Constantinople dans la literature slave contemporaine,' *Byzantinoslavica* XVII (1956) 278–340.

Dutu, A., and C. Cernovodeanu (edits.), *Dimitrie Cantemir, Historian of south-east European and Oriental civilizations* (Bucharest 1973).

Farmer, H.G., 'Turkish Artillery at the Fall of Constantinople,' *Transactions of the Glasgow University Oriental Society* VI (1929–33) 9–14.

Foss, C., and D. Winfield, *Byzantine Fortifications; an Introduction* (Pretoria 1986).

Hess, A.C., 'The Evolution of the Ottoman Seaborne Empire in the Age of Oceanic Discoveries, 1453–1525,' *American Historical Review* LXXV (1969–70) 1892–1919.

Housley, N.J., *The Later Crusades: from Lyons to Alcazar 1274–1580* (Oxford 1992).

Inalcik, H., 'Mehmed the Conqueror (1432–1481) and his Time,' *Speculum* XXXV (1960) 408–427.

Inalcik, H., *An Economic and Social History of the Ottoman Empire 1300–1914, vol. 1, 1300–1600* (London 1996).

Inalcik, H., *The Ottoman Empire: The Classical Age 1300–1600* (London 1973).

Iorga, N., 'Une source negligée de la prise Constantinople,' *Bulletin de la Section Historique (Acad. Roumaine)* XIII (1927) 59–68.

Káldy-Nagy, G., 'The First Centuries of the Ottoman Military Organization,' *Acta Orientalia Academiae Scientiarum Hungaricae* XXX (1977) 147–183.

Kiel, M., 'A Note on the History of the Frontiers of the Byzantine Empire in the 15th century,' *Byzantinische Zeitschrift* LXVI (1973), 351–353.

Langlois, V., 'Notice sur le sabre de Constantin XI, dernier empereur de Constantinople conservé à l'Armeria Reale de Turin,' *Revue Archeologique* XUV/1 (1857) 292–4.

Melville Jones, J.R., (trans.), *The Siege of Constantinople 1453: Seven Contemporary Accounts* (Amsterdam 1972).

Mihailovic, K. (edit. and trans. B. Stolz), *Memoires of a Janissary* (Ann Arbor 1975).

Mijatovich, C., *Constantine Palaeologus, The Last Emperor of the Greeks: 1448–1453: The Conquest of Constantinople by the Turks* (London 1892).

Nicol, D.M., *The End of the Byzantine Empire* (London 1979).

Nicol, D.M., *The Immortal Emperor* (London 1992).

Paviot, J., *Genoa and the Turks: 1444 and 1453* (Genoa 1988).

Pertusi, A., 'Le notizie sulla organizzazione administrativa e militare dei Turchi nello 'strategicon adversum Turcos' di Lampo Birago (c.1453–1455),' in *Studi sul medioevo cristiano offerti a R. Morghen* vol. II (Rome 1974) 669–700.

Philippides, M., (trans.), *Byzantium, Europe and the Early Ottoman Sultans, 1373–1513: An Anonymous Greek Chronicle of the Seventeenth Century (Codex Barberinus Graecus 111)* (New York 1990).

Philippides, M., (trans.), *The Fall of the Byzantine Empire: A Chronicle by George Sphrantzes 1401–1477* (Amherst 1980).

Pitcher, D.E., *An Historical Geography of the Ottoman Empire* (Leiden 1972).

Rolland, M., *Le siège de Constantinople 1453* (1989).

Runciman, S., *The Fall of Constantinople 1453* (Cambridge 1965).

Shaw, S., *History of the Ottoman Empire and Modern Turkey, vol. 1, 1280–1808* (Cambridge 1976).

Stacton, D., *The World on the Last Day* (London 1965).

Tafrali, O., 'Le siège de Constantinople dans les fresques des églises de Bucovine,' in *Melanges G. Schlumberger* (1924) 456–461.

Tsangadas, B.C.P., *The Fortifications and Defence of Constantinople* (New York 1980).

Turkova, H., 'Le Siège de Constantinople d'après le Seyahatname d'Evliya Celebi,' *Byzantinoslavica* XIV (1953) 1–13.

INDEX

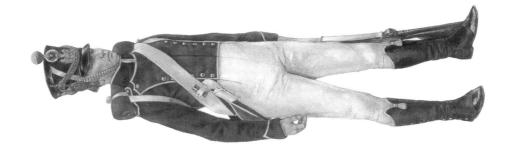

OSPREY PUBLISHING

FIND OUT MORE ABOUT OSPREY

❏ Please send me the latest listing of Osprey's publications

❏ I would like to subscribe to Osprey's e-mail newsletter

Title/rank

Name

Address

Postcode/zip   state/country

e-mail

I am interested in:

❏ Ancient world
❏ Medieval world
❏ 16th century
❏ 17th century
❏ 18th century
❏ Napoleonic
❏ 19th century

❏ American Civil War
❏ World War I
❏ World War II
❏ Modern warfare
❏ Military aviation
❏ Naval warfare

Please send to:

USA & Canada:
Osprey Direct USA, c/o MBI Publishing, P.O. Box 1, 729 Prospect Avenue, Osceola, WI 54020

UK, Europe and rest of world:
Osprey Direct UK, P.O. Box 140, Wellingborough, Northants, NN8 2FA, United Kingdom

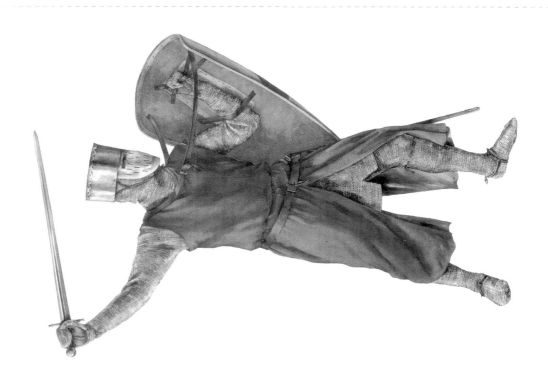

OSPREY
PUBLISHING

www.ospreypublishing.com

call our telephone hotline
for a free information pack

USA & Canada: 1-800-826-6600
UK, Europe and rest of world call:
+44 (0) 1933 443 863

Young Guardsman
Figure taken from *Warrior 22:
Imperial Guardsman 1799–1815*
Published by Osprey
Illustrated by Richard Hook

Knight, c.1190
Figure taken from *Warrior 1: Norman Knight 950 – 1204 AD*
Published by Osprey
Illustrated by Christa Hook

POSTCARD